ENVIRONMENTAL
MISSOURI

ISSUES AND SUSTAINABILITY
What You Need To Know

DON CORRIGAN

Webster
UNIVERSITY
Press

REEDY PRESS
St. Louis, Missouri

"*Environmental Missouri* is an essential reader for all who are concerned about the health and sustainability of human community in the region. Don Corrigan broadly surveys the range of our modern environmental degradations while introducing a host of engaged individuals who show us both how we depend on our environment and how we can care for it—well-researched, it is at the same time fluid and highly readable."
—David Lobbig, Curator of Environmental Life, Missouri History Museum

---

"Don Corrigan has written an incredibly important book that succeeds in describing many of our state's most complicated conservation issues in a very approachable way. All Missourians who care about the incredible natural resources of our great state should read Don's book in order to understand the challenges we face, and the work that needs to be accomplished. Don's history of covering environmental issues in Missouri gives his work great depth and provides important context for all those who work on environmental advocacy in the state of Missouri and beyond."
—Patricia Hagen, PhD, Executive Director / Vice President, Audubon Missouri

---

"*Environmental Missouri* is an enjoyable read packed full of great information and insights on Missouri's greatest environmental challenges. The author takes us on a journey through those issues in a way that is really easy to read. I especially liked the chapter ending expert Q &A's. Whether you are an environmentalist or just someone trying to get a handle on Missouri's natural world, I highly recommend reading this book."
—Larry Lazar, Citizen Advocate, Natural Resource Defense Council

---

"Don Corrigan has produced an easily navigated primer of brief, but comprehensive, explanations of the major environmental issues facing Missouri and the rest of the nation, fit for use as a jumping-off point for environment reporting students or the general public."
—Mark Schleifstein, Environment Reporter, NOLA.com /*The Times-Picayune*

"The environmental movement has needed a book like *Environmental Missouri* for a long time. Today, the environmental movement has fractured into a whole host of issues making it tough to keep track of each. Don Corrigan does a fantastic job presenting an even-handed and relevant introduction to these present day environmental issues. This is a must read for anyone interested in breathing fresh air, drinking clean water, and protecting the plants and animals that live in this world."
—Richard Thoma, President, Webster Groves Nature Study Society

"Don Corrigan's *Environmental Missouri* provides a comprehensive overview of the most pressing environmental challenges at play in the region. This book provides an important historic and geographic context that links our past, present and future environmental conditions. Its contents enable a greater understanding of the stakeholders, events and situations that local and regional environmental health advocates face on a daily basis. Interviews with local leaders and activists follow each chapter, adding a journalistic bent that brings diverse insider perspectives to the story. *Environmental Missouri* serves as an introduction and reference to those new to the environmental scene or new to the region, as it provides a valuable context that anchors work in Missouri's environmental sustainability sector."
—Cassandra P. Hage, Executive Director, St. Louis Earth Day

"Don Corrigan has put together a menu of daunting issues that still need solutions, with choices we still must make, and debates we all need to have. Today's environmental, energy, and climate challenges need knowledgeable and committed citizens to meet them. Citizens who understand the facts, the costs, the opportunities, and aren't afraid to debate, choose, and act—and demand action. No better introduction to that than Don's book, and no better place and people than the Show-Me State to make it happen."
—General (Ret.) Ron Keys, CNA Military Advisory Board Member, DOD Energy Security and Climate Change

"With perspective and facts, these essays lay out a broad range of environmental issues, specific to Missouri and also common in today's society overall. Understanding such problems contributes to both envisioning and enacting sustainable solutions, the alternatives needed to shift this issue-intensive status in our time—and for our planetary future."
—Jean Ponzi, St. Louis Environmental Educator and Advocate

"Here is a finely-crafted book in which serious issues are treated by Don Corrigan with a storytelling format that grabs the reader's attention. I read *Environmental Missouri* as both a concerned citizen and as a teacher. As a teacher and education consultant, my hope is that in the near future, we will see environmental education as an important part of curriculum in every school district—and this book is a good start to make that happen. *Environmental Missouri* motivates me, a concerned citizen, to get involved in local organizations addressing problems that should concern everybody."
—Beth Knoedelseder, Educator, Ladue School District

"Don Corrigan's latest book, *Environmental Missouri*, is a terrific snapshot of the myriad environmental issues facing the state. With this publication, Don has taken his gift for teaching environmental journalism—and inspiring students like me to become environmental journalists—to a much broader audience. The mosquito spraying chapter especially resonated, bringing back childhood memories of growing up in St. Louis County in the 1970s and running through the spray with friends on summer evenings, pretending we were in thick jungle fog. Corrigan's work highlights the remaining problems but also serves as a positive reminder of the progress made in the Show Me State."
—Dawn Reeves, Senior Correspondent, Inside EPA

"*Environmental Missouri* is a thorough, informative resource and a must-read for audiences interested in environmental issues, how climate change impacts daily life, and all fans of the Show-Me State's history. Don Corrigan's passion for educating on environmental issues is evident and continues to inspire my own personal environmental efforts."
—Andrea Harper, Coordinator, St. Louis Green, Inc.

"Informed by years of up-close observation as a newspaper reporter and editor, Don Corrigan has created a comprehensive primer on environmental issues affecting our region. Missouri truly has all the environmental issues, from A to Z, and Corrigan concisely digests them in this book, from river management issues to urban-suburban sprawl to industrial wastes and lifestyle decisions. He pulls no punches describing the negative, sometimes disastrous impacts of our environmental sins, but Corrigan also highlights solutions and positive trends in education, sustainable lifestyles, river cleanup efforts and even green burials. Environmental educators and citizens who want to be well informed on Missouri environmental issues will want to read this book."
—Emery Styron, Editor and Publisher, *River Hills Traveler*

Reedy Press

PO Box 5131

St. Louis, MO 63139

www.reedypress.com

Webster University Press

c/o Webster University Library

470 East Lockwood Avenue

St. Louis, MO 63119-3194

www.webster.edu/wup/

Library of Congress Control Number: 2014933255

ISBN: 978-1-935806-68-4

Design by Jill Halpin

Printed in the United States of America

13 14 15 16 17   5 4 3 2 1

CONTENTS

Preface   ix

SECTION I THE GOOD EARTH: RESPECTING OUR LAND

Rise and Fall of Urban Sprawl   4
McMansions: Neighborhood Monsters   9
Electromagnetic Fields   14
Rails to Trails   19
ATVs: Scarring Rural Countrysides   24
Clearcutting: Ozark Timber Terror   29
Trees Rediscovered: Tree City USA   34

SECTION II H20 IN THE MO: WATER ISSUES

Posted: "No Playing, Fishing, Swimming"   41
Beware: The "River Despair"   46
Meramec Mission: Operation Clean Stream   51
E. coli Clamor: Lake of the Ozarks   56
Asian Carp: Mississippi Invasives   61
Creve Coeur Lake: Wetlands Last Stand   66
Endangered: Ozark Scenic Waterways   71

SECTION III CLEAN AIR: A RIGHT, NOT A PRIVILEGE

Smog: Gets in Your Eyes and Lungs   78
Ozone: Twilight Toxic Zones   83
Lead: No Inhaling While Airborne   88
Airborne Mercury: Cryptic Contaminant   93
Sulfur Dioxide: Making Top Ten Lists   98
Mosquito Spraying: So Last Century   103
Smoking: The Ultimate Indoor Pollution   108

Section IV Toxics We Can Live Without

A Nuclear Burial Ground   115
Dioxin Sites: Ignorance Is Bliss   120
Coal Ash: A Fossil Fuel Flap   125
Getting the Lead (Poisoning) Out   130
Methane: Lighting Up Landfills   135
Plastics: Toxic to Fish and Fowl   140
PCBs: Detecting Damaging Data   145
Radon Gas: Invisible Menace   150

Section V Other State and National Issues

Radioactive Transport: Mobile Chernobyls?   158
CAFOs: Can You Smell That Smell?   163
GMOs and Labeling: A Food Fight   168
Pollinators Kaput: Colonies Collapsing   173
Hellbenders: Endangered Species   178
Power to the Parks People   183
Light Pollution: When Stars Don't Twinkle   188
Decibel Pollution: When Ears Do Not Hear   193

Section VI Show-Me Sustainability

Diaper Parties with Mrs. Sustainability   200
Pacific Ring's Mr. Sustainability   205
Greening Homes: Sufficiently Efficient   210
Alternative Energy: Gaining Power?   215
Rain Gardens and Rain Barrels, Oh My!   220
Clucking Over Backyard Chicken Coops   225
Green Education: Teaching Children Well   230
Green Burial: Sustainability at Trail's End   235

Appendix: Useful Environmental Resources   240

PREFACE

Environmental writer Mark Neuzil, a colleague of mine through our membership in the Society of Environmental Journalists (SEJ), has great yarns about his students at the University of St. Thomas. The Minnesota professor concedes that his students are bored silly by some environmental topics, but their interest level spikes when they hear about Ohio's Cuyahoga River fire in 1969. How could water catch on fire? This kind of question may boggle a young mind, but it also can inspire a lifelong interest in environmental protection and a career in environmental journalism and communication.

My own students at Webster University in St. Louis are similarly intrigued, astounded, and terribly curious about some of the bizarre environmental history and happenings here in the Show-Me State of Missouri. How could St. Louis allow coal smoke to get so bad that city street lights had to be turned on at noon? How did rail shipments of radioactive debris from the 1979 Three Mile Island disaster get routed through the major population centers of Kansas City and St. Louis? What possessed a waste hauler to spray dioxin-contaminated oil on the streets of a town known as Times Beach, necessitating its complete evacuation?

Sometimes it isn't enough to sit in a classroom to discuss and attempt to answer these questions about ecological hazards and environmental degradation. I will never forget the phone call I once received from the police chief of Eureka, Missouri, who explained that he had two of my journalism students in his jail. They had crossed the no-trespassing lines set up by the Environmental Protection Agency (EPA) around Times Beach. They trespassed in order to get close-up photos of what had become a dioxin-contaminated ghost town. "What do you want me to do with them?" the police chief inquired. I responded that he should let them cool their heels in his cell for a few hours longer. A short jail stay might be good experience for a career investigating stories that authorities would prefer to have covered from a distance.

My students' passion for environmental journalism has provided much of the inspiration for this book. Another motivating factor is the shortage of texts for this area of study. Quality books that do make sense for course adoption are still limiting because they tend to focus on a few topics at length, rather than offering a look at the great number of environmental issues available for discussion, research study, and expository writing. However, this book is not intended primarily for an academic setting. The book constitutes a sort of primer for "citizen journalists" and regular folks with an interest in what threats exist to their water, the air they breathe, and the places they inhabit.

One of the advantages for an author writing this kind of book in St. Louis is that the city and the state of Missouri have it all, from A to Z, when it comes to environmental problems. This was brought home to me in a big way in 1996 when 1,500 communicators with the Society of Environmental Journalists came to St. Louis and had several "field days" to study the region's environmental afflictions.

The SEJ convention offered a tour entitled "After the Bomb" to look at the role of St. Louis in nuclear weapons production and to examine the radioactive waste sites left behind in the Weldon Spring area. Another tour entitled "Dioxin Town Times Beach" involved a trip to the incinerator burning contaminated soil by the thousands of tons, under the supervision of the EPA. A full-day tour called "River Ecosystems" included a look back at the 500-year flood of 1993 and the unhealthy mold levels that can persist in structures long past decontamination efforts. After scrutiny of those efforts and the ecological impacts of mold spore contamination, the tour examined the future for flood management and river ecosystems in Missouri.

Of course, leaders in the St. Louis region and local tourism agencies were not exactly ecstatic over the idea of exposing out-of-town visitors to what might be described as the environmental underside, or the downside, of living in St. Louis and Missouri. For the same reason, these officials might not be so excited about this book, which catalogs some of the environmental issues facing the region. Nevertheless, I would argue that when you have a lot of lemons, make a lot of lemonade. The region really could capitalize on a new form of eco-tourism by laying out for visitors our environmental history and conundrums, as well as how these problems are being constructively addressed.

The St. Louis region and Missouri have some first-class universities and corporate institutions that are taking the initiative in studying and confronting serious environmental issues. Indeed, in that regard, the work of the St. Louis Zoo, St. Louis Science Center, Missouri Botanical Garden, Forest Park Forever and a myriad array of other environmental organizations receive mention in this book. They are cited for their efforts to make the region a cleaner, safer, and more ecologically friendly place to live. My hope is that this book not only interests readers, but also provides the impetus for establishing the region as a focal point and national site for a unique form of enviro-tourism.

ORGANIZATION OF THIS BOOK

This book is designed to be a general survey of environmental topics with the first three sections covering land issues, water issues, and air pollution issues. The treatment of these topics is not entirely academic or dispassionate, and that's because this writer has witnessed first-hand some of the protests over these environmental issues. Frankly, these events have provided some of the most engaging and enlightening moments for me as a weekly newspaper reporter and editor.

For example, the issue of McMansions brings to mind a long evening of taking notes in an unfamiliar living room, as neighbors consoled each other and also expressed outrage at developers building massive, in-fill monster homes on quiet streets. The rails-to-trails issue brings to mind a village meeting where residents worried about the litter, crime, and noise if an abandoned railroad track behind their homes was replaced with a hiking trail. Environmental concerns were a subplot in both of these local land-use dramas.

The water pollution issues covered in Section 2 and the air pollution issues in Section 3 also inspire reportorial recollections. Nothing is more confounding to me than covering clean stream operations year after year and witnessing the same boatloads of old tires and discarded appliances being fished out of Missouri rivers. When will rivers no longer be used as trash dumps and open sewers? For that matter, when will lawmakers enact

XII   ENVIRONMENTAL MISSOURI

tougher penalties for polluting both our water and our air? Environmental groups protest that politicians in recent years seem more intent on finding ways to relax standards for industrial pollution, rather than enforcing or strengthening laws.

Unfortunately, Missouri has a number of visible monuments to dangerous toxics produced in the state. To the south of St. Louis, there are the large mounds of lead tailings and abandoned smelters in the state's so-called "Lead Belt." To the west of St. Louis is the "pyramid" at Weldon Spring containing the radioactive debris from uranium processing for nuclear weapons. And throughout the St. Louis area are the towering landfills wrought by trash and waste hauling. Section 4 covers the toxics that make up these monuments, as well as dioxin, plastics, and PCBs.

Toxic wastes discussed in Section 4 can be ecologically destructive, endocrinologically disruptive, and just damned depressing. By contrast, Section 5 and Section 6 cover some issues that give cause for optimism. It's distressing to learn in Section 5 about endangered species such as Ozark hellbenders or the disappearing act of the honeybees. The good news is that zoologists and scientists are now making some progress to explain and address species loss. Likewise, it's disconcerting to learn in Section 5 about increases in noise and light pollution. The good news is that organizations like Noise Free America (NFA) and the International Dark-Sky Association (IDA) are increasing public awareness of these issues and promoting local, state, and national legislation to address them.

Sustainability is the focus of the final section of this book. In my experience, the people who populate the sustainability movement are reasonable, calm, and collected. Also, the multi-syllable word "sustainability" seems pretty benign to me. Yet, there exists a plethora of exercised critics eager to dismiss sustainability as either an innocuous buzzword or as the rallying cry of unwashed tree huggers promulgating a one-world, anti-development takeover of America.

My contention is that sustainability is neither superficial nor subversive. It's also here to stay for a couple of reasons: Young people like the idea of sustainability because it's grassroots and pragmatic. It can be practiced in the backyard or in the neighborhood. It's a way to make a difference without raising large amounts of money for a cause or demonstrating at the county government center. Also, businesses are embracing sustainability. They are adopting sustainability not only because it's good public relations, but because it can be good for the bottom line. From the business perspective, economic opportunities exist in the use of green building products, renewable energy sources, multi-modal transit, conservation management, and the use of renewable raw materials.

The final section examines ways in which advocates of green practices are bringing sustainability home, whether it's with solar panels on the roof, rain barrels connected to the downspouts, egg-laying chickens clucking behind the back porch, or the installation of energy-efficient windows and door frames. Section 6 also looks at how some individuals are seeking ways to be sustainable from the beginning of life to life's conclusion, from responsible choices for diapering baby to non-intrusive, low-impact green burials at the end of the trail.

ACKNOWLEDGMENTS

First of all, let's anticipate and acknowledge the inevitable critics of this work. The author is sympathetic with those who will argue that each topic in this book merits much more discussion and in-depth treatment. My response would be: Of course, but this collection of environmental topics is meant to be a starting point, not the final word or a definitive exposition. For students of environmental journalism, this collection offers a short introduction to a topic area with an invitation to explore the subject matter in much greater detail.

While I am offering mea culpas for my book approach in this preface, let me point out that the question-and-answer sections accompanying each topic are abbreviated. They were much more extensive in their original form and were pared down to meet the format requirements of this book. Inevitably some important content is sacrificed with this editing. Some reviewers also might find fault with the selection of "experts" that were chosen for the question-and-answer sections. Scientists might have been more suitable than activists as respondents on environmental topics.

For concerns about the expertise of selected respondents, it can be argued that many environmental issues come to the attention of the news media and the general public because of activists and concerned citizenry. They often provide the starting point for investigative journalism. They light the fire and keep it burning. It's then up to the professional communicators to sift through the embers and hot ash to find the core that burns true.

Finally, my hat is off to all those respondents in the book who took the time to answer the extensive question-and-answer surveys that I sent their way. I would additionally like to acknowledge the many environmental organizations that sent representatives to my college classes at Webster University to offer their perspectives on environmental issues. I drew from many of those sessions in constructing the topic areas of this book.

And, of course, I certainly must acknowledge my past, present, and future students in the Outdoor/Environmental Journalism Certificate classes at Webster University who are the reason for this book. Special thanks goes to Megan Favignano, who was extremely helpful with suggestions on editing and making this book more accessible for readers. Also, thanks to Julia Gabbert, who has always tried to keep me a more honest environmentalist with admonitions about recycling and breaking bottled water habits in the classroom.

Other students who have contributed in some way with my courses and this book include: Andrea Sisney, Max Bouvatte, Paul Kinker, Jennifer Proffitt, Akira Komatsu, Kendra Hicks, Andrea Harper, Stephanie Goggin, Edana Dillard, Albina Izmaylova, Jimmy Betts, Victoria Dickson, Olivia Bacott, Mary Eveker, Anthony Fairman, Erin Hindalong, Emam Saffof, Eleka Smith, John Pohl, Tierre Rhodes, Toni Thrasher, Ashley Westbrooke, Kaitlin Drake, Todd Schuessler, Eric Fuchs, Brandon Ferrell, Sheren Kahlel, Benjamin Wyckoff, and Holly Shanks.

Some very special photographers contributed their talents to this book. Award-winning photo journalist Diana Linsley, my colleague at the *Webster-Kirkwood Times*, provided sound advice and images. So did freelancers Max Bouvatte, Megan Favignano, Courtney Martin of Ella Bea Photography, Jill Moon of the *Alton Telegraph*, and several more. Their work is greatly appreciated.

ENVIRONMENTAL
MISSOURI

Section 1

THE GOOD EARTH
RESPECTING OUR LAND

"Not all change is progress. America is losing 7,000 acres daily to development. Most of our wetlands are already lost. The farms and ranches that helped define who we are as a people are being pushed farther and farther out, out of sight and out of mind. Many of our cities and towns lack green spaces that are the source for physical recreation and spiritual re-creation."

—Will Rogers, President
The Trust for Public Land, 1999

A t some point in their careers, many community reporters come to realize that they have evolved into environmental journalists. They are writing stories about land use. They are talking to concerned citizens who are asking environmental questions about where they live. These citizens ask: Do we really want to give up more green space for a strip mall or condo complex? Do we really want another ribbon of concrete through our town to speed up the daily commute?

Many of the issues covered in this book, and especially in this section, came to this journalist's attention during more than a score of years of community reporting. The term "McMansion" was bandied about at a neighborhood meeting of residents who'd had enough of real estate mayhem on their streets. Modest homes were being bulldozed to make way for monster abodes with multi-car garages.

The acronym "EMFs" lit up the room at a heated meeting of neighbors upset over high-tension power lines coming through their backyards on giant electric towers. The environmental threat was more than just aesthetic, according to the residents. They insisted the electromagnetic fields (EMFs) from the power lines presented a community health issue.

Not all land-use issues, however, involve NIMBY (Not In My Backyard) controversies. Sometimes urban, suburban, and ex-urban residents are raising voices about what is happening fifty or one hundred miles away. They are concerned about "no woods left behind" for youngsters because of poor land management and forestry practices miles from where they live. They are concerned about ATVs (All-Terrain Vehicles) ripping up the land and destroying habitat for creatures that aren't equipped with mud flaps and deep-tread wheels.

RISE AND FALL OF
URBAN
SPRAWL

Photo by Max Bouvatte

A popular joke at the time of the 1985 I-70 World Series between the St. Louis Cardinals and the Kansas City Royals was that it wouldn't be too long before the baseball clubs' metro areas met in Columbia, Missouri. Three decades later that was not so much of a joke, as the St. Louis metro area stretched to Lake St. Louis, Wentzville, and Warrenton; and the Kansas City metro area stretched to Lee's Summit, Independence, and Blue Springs.

All of this expansion would be understandable if it was organic and the result of a burgeoning economy. Unfortunately, this growth is the consequence of a pattern of growth known as urban sprawl. Sprawl has hurt the essential core areas of both St. Louis and Kansas City, because their tax bases have suffered as the affluent move farther and farther out from the urban centers. Residential and commercial development often follows the exodus from cities.

Additional downsides to urban sprawl from an environmental standpoint can be even more alarming. Residents in areas of urban sprawl generate more carbon emissions per capita than urban dwellers because of their reliance on automobile transportation. An increase in highway pavement and parking lots results in excessive runoff from precipitation, which pollutes lakes, streams, and water sources. Highways and sprawling development not only eliminate habitat for plants and animals, but also can seriously interrupt migration patterns that have a global impact on species.

Public policy experts and sociologists see pernicious effects on the human species. Critics of sprawl talk about a decline in "social capital" in low-density suburbs, as residents often have less interaction with neighbors and lose public spaces in which to congregate and converse.[1] Simultaneously, reliance on a car-centered culture has the effect of reducing exercise from walking or bicycling. Inhabitants must drive everywhere in far-flung suburbs, which health experts blame for a rise in obesity and related maladies such as diabetes, hypertension, and heart problems.

Critics and Defenders Spar Over Sprawl

There's no shortage of environmental groups that have spoken out against urban sprawl and a general lack of public policy to discourage such growth. The Sierra Club and the Audubon Society have opposed sprawl and encouraged living styles that cut down on automobile use and that also are less intrusive on nature.[2]

Inner-ring suburbs and outer-ring suburbs have plenty of vocal defenders as well, who view suburban living as the fulfillment of the American Dream. Conservative and libertarian policy institutes argue that freedom in America includes the freedom to choose where one wishes to live—and choosing the suburbs can be due to a preference for better schools, less crime, more privacy, less noise, and more contact with the outdoors on a comfortable deck out back.[3]

Urban Sprawl Has a Price Tag

Alex Ihnen, a public affairs blogger and chair of City To River in St. Louis, said it's all well and good for the Cato Institute and others to cheer on the flight to the suburbs. However, he thinks they should also support an end to tax money subsidizing urban sprawl. The enormous costs for new highways, public sewers, utilities, and other infrastructure should be borne by the developers who build subdivisions far from existing services.

Todd Swanstrom, a professor of public policy at the University of Missouri–St. Louis, agreed with Ihnen that there are unanticipated costs to sprawl. He said a tight economy, however, is opening some eyes to the tab for sprawl and the tax dollars needed to sustain it.

"One big problem with sprawl is the amount of impervious surface that is created with highways and parking lots," said Swanstrom. "This results in run-off, erosion, water pollution issues and flash flooding. And the taxpayers get hit to try to fix these problems, not developers."[4]

Smart Growth and New Urbanism

According to Swanstrom, the realization that there is a social, economic, and environmental cost to sprawl is not the only factor working against further expansion from city centers. He said a younger generation has taken up the cause of greener, more energy-efficient, higher-density living and pedestrian-friendly lifestyles.

"There are two trends that young people are embracing," said Swanstrom. "There is the 'new urbanism' that militates against the big-box shopping malls with vast parking lots. There's also the 'smart growth movement,' which works toward wiser use of energy and less reliance on fossil fuel consumption. The fact that there is now a 'walkability index' in St. Louis and other cities to judge the value of living in various neighborhoods is a clue to what is going on."[5]

Urban Sprawl Q & A

Alex Ihnen is the editor of nextSTL.com, which covers subjects from historic preservation to public policy. He is also the chair of City To River in St. Louis, an organization that works to reopen the Mississippi riverfront to the city.

Q. Why should environmentalists care about urban sprawl? How has it contributed to pollution problems? Is it because of long commutes and car dependency?

A. The impact of sprawl is most concerning as a question of utilizing resources, physical and monetary. There is added pollution, the lengthening commutes and other car trips, but also inefficient single-family homes and stand-alone restaurants and stores. There's also an exceptionally high cost associated with maintaining highways and other roads as well as expansive parking lots.

Q. As we've seen construction of two new super malls in the urban sprawl area of far west St. Louis County, what effects might these developments have on water pollution, water run-off, flash flooding?

A. The two malls in question each have thousands of square feet of impermeable surface parking lots. They're both located in a floodplain that was underwater during the 1993 flood. Run-off will be concentrated and faster flowing, will carry more pollutants from automobiles and trash from people.

Q. How would you rank in order the top five deleterious effects of sprawl (pollution, car-dependency, increased obesity, decreased social capital, strip mall culture, infrastructure costs, segregation, etc.)?

A. I'd put decreased social capital at the top and far above other concerns as I believe that it is the root cause of other negative side effects. A community with healthy social capital (and thus perhaps healthy civic engagement) will more success-fully address other issues. In a basic sense, infrastructure costs will hamper us for decades and development will continue to migrate around the region, attracted by relative bargains, while aging infrastructure will be abandoned (see MSD sewer/water issues) and paid for by relatively few people.

Q. Americans, especially now, seem to whine about the nanny state when any restrictions are imposed on sprawl (or big gulps). How do you answer libertarians from Cato and elsewhere who say low-density is a preferred lifestyle and freedom of choice to live where we want must be defended?

A. I would wholeheartedly agree with the Cato Institute and ask them to then stop supporting the subsidization of sprawl. They should be against funding highway expansion, road widening projects, and other infrastructure. If someone wishes to live in Ballwin, Missouri, that's their right; however, they should pay the cost of living there.

Q. What factors make sprawl in the St. Louis region peculiar or especially pronounced as compared to some other urban areas in the U.S. and the world?

A. The defining characteristic in St. Louis is the fragmented nature of our sprawl. As of June 2012, there are ninety municipalities in St. Louis County, averaging fewer than 7,500 residents. This has happened largely due to residents' desire to control zoning as a means to enforcing racial and economic segregation following World War II.

Notes

1. Cato Institute: "Critiquing Sprawl's Critics," www.cato.org/sites/cato.org/files/pubs/pdf/pa365.pdf.
2. Sierra Club on Building Better, www.sierraclub.org/sprawl/report05/buildingbetter.pdf.
3. Infed.org: Robert Putnam: Social Capital and Civic Community, www.infed.org/thinkers/putnam.htm.
4. Corrigan, Don, "Commercial Musical Chairs," *Webster-Kirkwood Times* (January 4, 2013): 14.
5. Ibid.

Additional Readings

Bruegmann, Robert, *Sprawl: A Compact History* (Chicago: University of Chicago Press, 2005).
Jackson, Kenneth T., *Crabgrass Frontier: The Suburbanization of the United States* (New York: Oxford University Press, 1985).
Hayden, Dolores, *A Field Guide to Sprawl* (New York: W.W. Norton & Co., 2004).
Hirschhorn, Joel S., *Sprawl Kills: How Blandburbs Steal Your Time, Health, and Money* (New York: Sterling & Ross, 2005).
Putnam, Robert, *Bowling Alone* (New York: Touchstone Books, 2001).

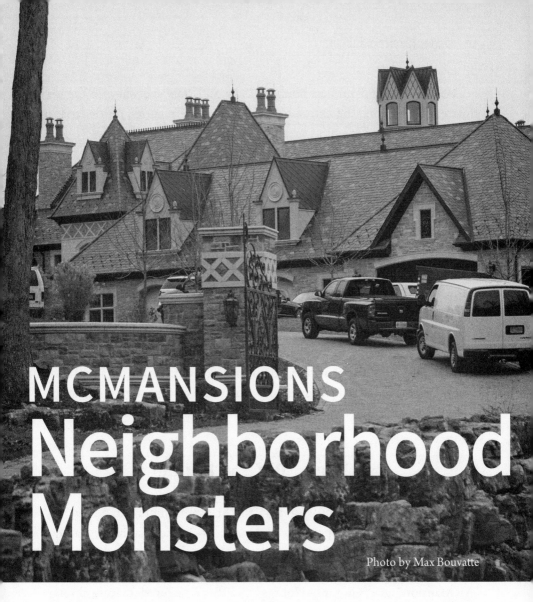

MCMANSIONS
Neighborhood Monsters

Photo by Max Bouvatte

B efore the home construction bubble burst with the economic crash of 2008, new luxury houses sprouted up like daisies across the U.S. landscape for two decades—and Missouri was no exception to all this sprouting. In established neighborhoods, older homes here and there were mowed down to make way for newer, larger, more ostentatious residences. This phenomenon was tagged derisively as the "McMansion" trend by property owners who opposed behemoths changing the character and culture of their residential areas.

A massive $26.7 million home in Lake St. Louis evolved into the ultimate McMansion. The extravagant home was the planned residence for Darain Atkinson of an auto warranty company known as U.S. Fidelis, and was monumental in its excess. The monster home at 5 Lakeview Court, situated in a suburban tract of neatly kept yards and 1970s ranch houses, became the focal point of numerous stories on mindless American extravagance. Even more articles about the McMansion cropped up after Atkinson was charged with fraud and later sentenced to eight years in prison.[1]

Most news media stories about McMansions don't involve houses with their own bowling alley, beauty salon, art studio, exercise area, meditation tower, and seven-car garage. Most news stories about McMansions are about zoning ordinances, land-use covenants, planning officials, a determined developer, and some very upset neighbors saying, "There goes the neighborhood!" Some environmental types may also be in the mix. They stress that McMansions are a byproduct of urban sprawl, a detriment to natural surroundings, and a poor investment for the future as a younger generation looks for sustainable living and lifestyles, not symbols of wealth and success.

Battling a "Big Bad Builder"

A McMansion fight broke out in the St. Louis suburb of Kirkwood in 2006 when a developer tore down his own modest home in the subdivision of Craig Woods to build a much larger home on the same plot. His plans prompted an angry homeowners meeting in which terms like "McMansion" and "Hummer Houses" and "Big Bad Builder" were among many discouraging words bandied about. Upset neighbors did not want to see their California-style, mid-century ranch homes interrupted by a "Garage Mahal."

"We've got a neighborhood with great character and a significant architectural style," said Tom Burke of Craig Woods. "The homes are modest, built with organic materials—lots of wood and stone—with low-pitched roofs that fit in with the natural setting. We have a subdivision board of trustees with covenants that have held up for fifty years to protect the look of our neighborhood. Now, a developer flaunts the covenants; demolishes what's been here; and builds an in-your-face monster house that screams out: 'Look at us—we've got ours, Jack!'"[2]

The neighbors appealed to city officials in Kirkwood to have the city attorney enforce their covenants and to stop the in-fill McMansion house. However, the city attorney balked at this idea and said the city had no standing to enforce their covenants. He said if property owners want to get together to establish architectural styles and restrict land uses for their neighborhood, then more power to them, but they must hire their own attorneys to enforce their regulations.[3]

Demise of the McMansion Trend?

Ultimately, the economic downturn beginning in 2008 has had more of an impact on slowing down the McMansion trend than any move toward more local regulations. McMansions do not appeal to younger families because they have lost their attraction as a solid investment, and even more important, their practicality. As St. Louis land-use expert and architectural historian Esley Hamilton observes: "Today's big houses for the most part lack any practical justification, as families have become smaller, servants have disappeared, and formal entertaining, if it exists at all, has moved from the home to specialized locations."

McMansions Q & A

Esley Hamilton has been the preservation historian for St. Louis County Parks & Recreation in Missouri for more than thirty years. One of his responsibilities is to survey historic buildings in the county and to nominate outstanding specimens for recognition on the National Register of Historic Places.

Q. How are McMansion houses problematic and at odds with the growing sustainability movement?

A. Today's big houses for the most part lack any practical justification. The McMansions that have caused the most comment have been the ones built to replace smaller, older houses in communities such as Webster Groves, Kirkwood, Clayton, Ladue, and Olivette.

Q. How do you respond to those who say it's "nanny zoning" for a city or county to restrict McMansions? Shouldn't owners be allowed to do what they want with their land?

A. The introduction of an over-scaled house into a neighborhood reduces the value of every other house in the neighborhood. The effect is often the same as racial blockbusting was in the 1950s—everybody in a smaller house sells and moves out. Shouldn't government protect the value of its citizens' homes?

Q. What should an "In-fill Housing Committee" in a city or county actually study and act upon when it comes to McMansions?

A. It seems late to be entering this arena now after so many years of this phenomenon, but if this is the case, the necessary regulatory tools are already available in some communities that can be used as models: demolition delays, architectural design review, setbacks, height limitations, and floor-area ratios.

Q. Has the 2008 economic crash put a crimp in the McMansion trend? Or will increased concentration of wealth since 2008 mean more McMansions in the future?

A. The National Trust has observed a slowdown in McMansions in the past few years. The financial logic (if any) of a McMansion is based on the assumption that property values will continue to rise and that they'll rise more for big houses than for small ones.

Since 2007 we have been reminded that this assumption is not always true. In St. Louis, the decline in real estate values has been very uneven, so that in the most fashionable parts of the metro area, property values have continued to rise. This has meant, in some cases, that some houses that might have been targets for teardowns a few years ago are now too expensive to tear down.

Q. Darain Atkinson's (U.S. Fidelis) $26.7 million home has been called the "ultimate McMansion." Is there a moral dimension to this kind of conspicuous consumption, and does it symbolize McMansion development on steroids?

A. The Darain Atkinson saga is just the latest chapter in a typically American phenomenon. Samuel Insull built the Chicago Civic Opera House for his wife and then had to flee the country when his business collapsed in the Depression. If you allow for inflation, other houses in the St. Louis region must have been nearly as expensive, including several of the houses on Vandeventer Place and country houses such as Grant's Farm. The contrast between the Atkinson House and its setting tells more about the failure of leadership in Lake St. Louis than it does about Atkinson.

Notes

1. Patrick, Robert, "Eight Years in Prison for U.S. Fidelis Co-Founder," *St. Louis Post-Dispatch* (September 22, 2012): A1.
2. Corrigan, Don, "Ranch House, Ranch House—Boom! McMansion," *Webster-Kirkwood Times* (March 10, 2006): 1.
3. Ibid.

Additional Readings

Bruegmann, Robert, *Sprawl: A Compact History* (Chicago: University of Chicago Press, 2005).
Etzioni, Amitai, *Spirit of Community* (New York: Touchstone Books, 1994).
Flint, Anthony, *The Battle Over Sprawl and the Future of America* (Baltimore: Johns Hopkins Press, 2006).

ELECTROMAGNETIC FIELDS

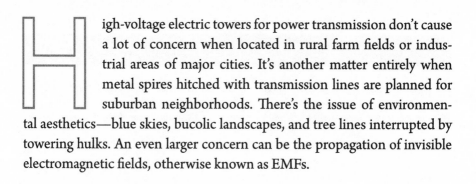

Photo by Megan Favignano

H igh-voltage electric towers for power transmission don't cause a lot of concern when located in rural farm fields or industrial areas of major cities. It's another matter entirely when metal spires hitched with transmission lines are planned for suburban neighborhoods. There's the issue of environmental aesthetics—blue skies, bucolic landscapes, and tree lines interrupted by towering hulks. An even larger concern can be the propagation of invisible electromagnetic fields, otherwise known as EMFs.

In 1993, the St. Louis suburb of Webster Groves became the focal point of an EMF controversy when residents learned that Union Electric (now Ameren) had a plan to erect more than two dozen 100-foot utility poles in their community. Linda Fasterling, an Avery School Elementary teacher, heard about the plan from one of her student's parents. As the word spread, about thirty to forty residents decided to meet together to discuss the utility line issue, and soon a grassroots environmental group was formed. They named themselves CURE, Citizens United for Responsible Energy.

"CURE was not advocating for a decrease in available electricity but a responsible use of electricity by consumers and the companies that provide it," said Fasterling. "We understood the need to increase the availability of electricity, but we were questioning why it had to be run through or along residential neighborhoods."

Concern Over Electromagnetic Fields

Webster Groves is only one of many communities across the nation that have wrestled with the issue of EMFs and what health hazards are posed by their presence, particularly for youngsters. Other metro areas where alarms have been raised include Denver, Portland, San Diego, and more.[1] The EMF issue is also a global concern with research studies on the effects of EMFs having been conducted in Australia, Brazil, Canada, Finland, Germany, Sweden, Taiwan, and the United Kingdom.[2]

EMFs are measured in milligaus (mg). European studies conclude that regular exposure to even low milligaus levels can lead to increased rates of breast cancer, brain cancer, and leukemia.[3] According to CURE, Swedish scientists found that children exposed to power line fields of more than 1 mg experienced twice the risk of developing leukemia as children exposed to less than 1 mg. Those exposed to 2 mg had nearly three times the risk, and those living in fields of 3 mg, almost four times the risk.[4] CURE activists noted that Missouri's Union Electric Company estimated milligaus rates on some properties near the proposed lines would exceed 6 mg.

In covering the power line battle in suburban St. Louis, the *St. Louis Post-Dispatch* summed up the national and international studies on the health effects of EMFs in its news analysis page: "Some of the thousands of scientific reports since 1980 suggest that EMFs from power lines and other electrical equipment may contribute to cancer and other health problems. Many other studies found no such link. The utility industry and many scientists in and out of the industry say the evidence of a health threat is unclear."[5]

EMFs: Not Just a Power Line Controversy

Activists with CURE lost their battle with the local utility, and the transmission line was built. To this day, most CURE members remain wary of power lines and say they are tired of hearing that studies on the effects of EMFs are inconclusive. They believe that high-voltage lines should be buried to reduce EMF exposure and to provide more reliable electricity. Utilities argue that burying lines would be expensive and would raise electricity costs. In the meantime, new concerns about EMF exposure have been raised because of widespread use of cell phone technology.[6]

EMFs Q & A

Linda Fasterling is a founding member of Citizens United for Responsible Energy (CURE). CURE has advocated for rational policies on the use of electricity by consumers and providers. She has a BS in Physical Education and (K-12) teaching experience. Fasterling is originally from New York. Her three children all graduated from Webster Groves High School in Webster Groves, Missouri.

Q. American scientific studies on the impact of EMFs (electromagnetic fields) usually downplay or dismiss the dangers from power lines as compared to the European studies on EMFs. What do you think accounts for this?

A. Personally, Americans are quick to jump onboard anything the government says is "okay." No one, even today, wants to think that something as necessary as electricity could have unintended health consequences. We want it fast, cheap, and in a steady supply, regardless of where the lines need to be run.

Q. Some CURE members became more observant about the presence of power lines on school properties and in lower income areas. They researched to find milligaus rates for EMFs to be very high on these properties. What conclusions might be drawn from that?

A. My job, at the time (CURE was most active), was to contact people and groups mentioned in Paul Brodeur's book *The Great Power-Line Cover-Up*.

One of the women I talked to said, "Watch what the power companies do with the land under the power lines. They sell it to low-income groups or communities for little or no money or they rent it to them for next to nothing."

Cities are often desperate for low-cost options, and desperate cities take desperate measures. No one, unless they're aware of the health concerns, is going to question the offer of low-cost land. The city thinks the utility is being benevolent, and the utility walks away with a purchase price or long-term rent.

Q. Much of the concern on EMFs now seems to be focused on the impact of cell phones, music earbuds, and excessive use of e-tablets and home computers. Are these bigger concerns to you now than the whole power line controversy?

A. If researching the issue of EMFs brings you to make decisions regarding use of those objects, then so be it. I don't believe the final word has been written on anything that causes brain waves to alter.

Q. What is a positive solution to the power line controversy? Solar panels, geothermal, or alternative power that does not require massive transmission lines and facilities? Should lines be buried?

A. Cities are realizing they can produce much of their own electricity through solar, geothermal, and wind to reduce their dependence on "the grid." Burying lines can be an effective alternative to running local power lines, if they're encased properly.

Notes

1. Krieger, Roy, "On the Line," *American Bar Association Journal* (January 1994): 40.
2. Adamsak, Phil, "EMF Controversy," *Visions* (Summer 1992): 7.
3. McManus, T., *Electromagnetic Fields: Report to Mr. Robert Molloy. T.D., Minister for Energy, Ireland* (Ireland: Department of Energy, 1992), 102-108.
4. Harris, Deborah, "CURE Meeting Intensifies Concerns on EMFs," *Webster-Kirkwood Times* (November 26, 1993): 4.
5. Allen, William, "Battle Lines," *St. Louis Post-Dispatch* (November 28, 1993): B1.
6. Davis, Devra, *Disconnect: The Truth About Cell Phone Radiation* (New York: Penguin, 2010), 1-50.

Additional Readings

Brodeur, Paul, *The Great Power-Line Cover-Up: How the Utilities and the Government Are Trying to Hide the Cancer Hazard Posed by Electromagnetic Fields* (Boston: Little, Brown and Co., 1993).
Brodeur, Paul, "The Hazards of Electromagnetic Fields II—Something Is Happening," *The New Yorker* (June 19, 1989): 47.
Park, Robert, *Voodoo Science: The Road from Foolishness to Fraud* (New York: Oxford University Press Inc., 2000).

RAILS TO
TRAILS

Photo by Megan Favignano

A great American success story in the archives of national land use history involves the rails-to-trails movement. Literally hundreds of miles of abandoned railroad track have been converted for recreational use, much to the great pleasure of bikers, hikers, joggers, in-line skaters, as well as nature lovers and environmentalists. The transformation of these frayed ribbons of railroad company land for outdoor activities has not come without a price, without political obstacles, and without a bit of controversy.

Case in point: Grant's Trail in southwest St. Louis County. Named for President Ulysses S. Grant, who once resided in the area, the trail project was under the oversight of Ted Curtis, executive director of Gateway Trailnet during the 1990s and into the new century. Much of the trail would be built in the middle of a one hundred-foot railroad right-of-way. Old railroad ties would be removed and the trail would consist of twelve-foot-wide paving with crushed rock at the sides.

The trail was built in segments, but before any construction could begin, intricate negotiations were necessary with entities ranging from the federal government to St. Louis County to small cities like Crestwood, Oakland, Grantwood Village, and more. At city meetings, the omnipresent NIMBY (Not In My Backyard) residents complained about parking issues, noise, litter, vagrants, burglars, and any other unwanted phenomena that the trail might bring.

"There isn't a rails-to-trails project in the country that hasn't had to deal with problems like this," said Ted Curtis in 1998, after facing a barrage of criticism over where trail users would park. Condo resident Nina Nolan said she looked forward to walking her dog, Schnitzel, on the trail, but she was afraid trail users would fill up her condo parking lot with their vehicles.[1] Eight years later in 2006, despite all the obstacles, a full eight miles of trail became available from Reavis Barracks and I-55 to Kirkwood near I-44.

Katy: Missouri's Ultimate Rail Conversion

The task of converting portions of abandoned Union Pacific railroad track for eight miles of Ulysses S. Grant Trail was a daunting undertaking. Imagine the challenge of developing 240 miles of trail across the state of Missouri in the right-of-way of the former Missouri-Kansas-Texas Railroad. The familiar nickname "Katy" for the Katy Trail comes from the pronunciation of the initials of the railroad known as the MKT.[2] Thirty times the length of Grant's Trail, the Katy may well have encountered thirty times the headaches in its crushed limestone road to completion.

Among the impediments to completing the Katy Trail were periodic flooding and harsh weather, acquisition and maintenance of bridges, demands for safety fences, enforcement of day-use-only policies, requirements for patrolling by commissioned officers—and 240 miles of construction costs. Add to all of this the lawsuits by adjacent landowners, who argued that if the rail line was no longer in use, the property should rightfully revert to them. They became part of the National Association of Reversionary Property Owners (NARPO), a group that also claimed that trails devalue their property.[3]

Trails: An Environmentalist's Best Friend

In spite of all the opposition, the Katy Trail celebrated its twentieth anniversary in 2010. The anniversary was a time to reflect on the challenges faced by Missouri State Parks to complete the trail, and to honor those who made the trail possible—people like Ted and Pat Jones, who donated the initial $2.2 million needed to acquire the corridor and to begin construction.[4]

"We continue to receive support from organizations like the Edward Jones investment company, Missouri Department of Transportation, the Missouri State Parks Foundation, and the Katy Land Trust," noted Dawn Fredrickson, field operations & Katy Trail coordinator with Missouri State Parks under the Department of Natural Resources (DNR).

Environmentalists know that trails are their best friends, because trail users who enjoy the scenery become advocates for nature protection and environmentalism. According to Fredrickson, some of the best scenery on the Katy includes a St. Charles section (milepost 39.5) where the trail runs parallel to the Missouri River; a section between Bernheimer (milepost 89) and Gore (93.8) with magnificent views of the river and towering bluffs; a section between Portland (milepost 115.9) and Mokane (milepost 125), which is densely forested; a section between McBaine (milepost 169.5) and Rocheport (178.3), with river bluffs and a state champion bur oak tree.

Fredrickson's personal favorite is the section of the trail between Pilot Grove (milepost 203.3) and Clifton City (milepost 215.4). This area is heavily wooded and moderately hilly, with rock outcroppings of Ozark-type topography.

Rails to Trails Q&A

Dawn Fredrickson is the field operations & Katy Trail coordinator. She oversees the entire trail's funding and staffing to ensure the trail is maintained. She also works to protect the trail's resources.

Q. Recreational trails from Grant's Trail in the St. Louis region to the Katy Trail across Missouri have replaced old railroad routes. How did this happen?

A. In 1983, Congress amended the National Trails System Act to provide for the railbanking of railroad corridors that were no longer in use by railroad companies. "Railbanking" is a term that describes the voluntary agreement between a railroad company proposing to abandon a railroad right-of-way and a trail sponsor interested in converting it to a recreational trail. While being used as a trail, the railroad corridor is "banked" for the future, should a railroad company want to restore its use as a railroad.

Q. What is the 1968 National Trails System Act (NTSA), and what are the three categories of national trails?

A. Congress established the Outdoor Recreation Resources Review Commission (ORRRC) in 1958 to study outdoor recreation use, inventory existing recreational facilities, and project needed recreational facilities for the future. The commission's recommendations also resulted in several other interesting initiatives for outdoor recreation, including the 1968 National Trails System Act, which established a nationwide system of trails that fall into one of three categories— National Scenic Trail, National Historic Trail and National Recreation Trail.

Q. NIMBYs opposed the Grant's Trail rails-to-trails conversion in St. Louis's South County for fear of noise, litter, and crime. Now these neighbors seem to see it as an asset. Did any of this go on with the Katy?

A. There was some pretty outspoken opposition to the trail when it was first being proposed in 1986. Understandably, many of the landowners along the MKT corridor felt that, if the rail line was no longer in use, the land should revert back to them. Several of these landowners initiated lawsuits that challenged the constitutionality of the Railbanking Amendment. In 1990, the U.S. Supreme Court upheld the constitutionality of railbanking but also made provision for compensating landowners.

Q. How are trails a good investment for taxpayers?

A. Taking a rail corridor that is no longer in use and converting it to a long-distance recreational trail promotes tourism, which is a boon for those railroad communities that no longer receive income derived from an active railroad. We've seen this on the Katy Trail with the establishment of businesses and services that cater specifically to trail users.

Q. What is the biggest threat to the continued existence of the Katy?

A. The biggest threat to the Katy Trail is one that is experienced by all Missouri state parks and state historic sites. The Missouri State Park system is fortunate in that we're funded by a 1/10 of 1 percent sales tax—the Parks, Soils and Water Sales Tax. Because we don't have user fees, the Katy Trail is primarily funded through the sales tax and through donations.

   If we lose relevance with the citizens of the state and aren't able to demonstrate the importance of preserving the state's outstanding natural and cultural resources, Missouri's citizenry will no longer support the sales tax—which is why it is critical for us to be responsive to our constituents and show that we are being good stewards of Missouri's estate.

Notes

1. Corrigan, Don, "Federal Monies on Hold for Paving, More Parking Along Grant's Trail," *South County Times* (October 2, 1998): 1.
2. Trail History and Features at Katy Trail State Park, mostateparks.com/page/57943/trail-history-and-features.
3. National Association of Reversionary Property Owners, home.earthlink.net/~dick156.
4. Zagier, Alan Scher, "Katy Trail Seen as Success 20 Years After Opening," *Columbia Missourian* (May 4, 2010).

Additional Readings

Dufur, Brett, *The Complete Katy Trail Guidebook* (Rocheport, Mo.: Pebble Publishing, 2002).
Rails to Trails Conservancy, www.railstotrails.org/news/newsroom/index.html.
Richardson, Shawn, *Biking Missouri's Rail-Trails: Where to Go, What to Expect, How to Get There* (Minnesota: Adventure Publications, 1999).
"Surface Transportation: Issues Related to Preserving Inactive Rail Lines as Trails," www.gao.gov/new.items/rc00004.pdf.

ATVs
SCARRING RURAL COUNTRYSIDES

A ll-terrain vehicles, otherwise known as ATVs, can be ridden just about everywhere: on farms, on trails, on shorelines, on prairies, in forests, in creeks, and in streams. ATV enthusiasts would probably ride them on the moon if transport to the lunar surface was available, but ATV critics are unhappy enough about terrestrial ATV use. These critics fear that unrestricted ATV use on the earth's surface could actually leave an environment resembling a cratered, lunar landscape.

The off-road vehicles, with their low-pressure tires, scooped seats designed for straddling, and wide handlebars for steering, are the ultimate motorized machine for tackling unpaved terrain. Midwest Trail Riders Association (MTRA) members love their ATVs and revel in their versatility. After all, they provide the freedom to go "off the beaten path," to engage in recreational racing activities, and to explore the great outdoors with a minimum of physical exertion.[1]

Opponents of ATVs, such as the Norbeck Society, can provide an endless list of the damaging environmental effects of ATV use. Among the effects are sedimentation and compaction of the soil; damage to native vegetation and the spread of weeds and invasives; loss of habitat for both plant and animal species; and pollution of air, water, and land areas. Pollution from ATVs has been known to poison plants and obstruct photosynthesis, weakening plants to disease and to succumbing to the encroachment of invasives.[2]

All-terrain vehicles have become popular among hunters and anglers, because ATVs can quickly take them to previously inaccessible sites. However, observant anglers have reported a decline in fish populations in the vicinity of ATV use, just as serious hunters also have described a loss of game species in areas where ATV use has proliferated.[3]

Restrictions Difficult to Enforce

Rider safety seems to be the primary focus of ATV regulations in Missouri with riders under eighteen required to wear helmets, and helmet use greatly encouraged for those over eighteen. Although a driver's license is required for ATV use on country roads and on some dedicated park trails, it's not uncommon to find youngsters operating ATVs illegally in the state. Safety concerns have increased nationwide in recent years, because of hundreds of deaths and thousands of injuries involving ATVs as reported by the Consumer Product Safety Commission.[4]

In Missouri, ATV riders are advised to only stay on dedicated trails and to resist the temptation to ride through streams and creeks. The Chadwick area of the Mark Twain National Forest, which offers trails for motorcycle and ATV use, has special orange markers to indicate where such vehicles are permitted. A 2006 law in Missouri takes into account some environmental considerations and prohibits ATVs in creeks and streams.[5] However, regulations are difficult to enforce. There are simply not enough conservation agents and park rangers to monitor illegal ATV use in the state's wild areas.

Deep Ecology Movement and ATVs

The so-called Deep Ecology Movement in America has taken aim at the widespread use of ATVs and other off-road vehicles (ORV) in America. David Orton, who has developed a concept known as "biocentrism" within the movement, has said environmentalists intent on imposing new restrictions on ATVs have got it wrong. He believes environmentalists must demand that ATVs and ORVs be banned for any recreational purposes.

"We must move our definitions of self away from the acquisition of consumer goods and open people's eyes to the damage done by such machines to the natural world," writes Orton. "We need fundamental change . . . this change should start by realizing that putting a down payment on an ORV (a high-end ATV can cost more than $12,000 per unit; a snowmobile can retail for over $10,000) does not give one the right of entry to nature, let alone the right to aid in her destruction."[6]

ATV Impact Q & A

George Wuerthner is an ecologist involved with America's Deep Ecology Movement. He has an interest in public land issues and has traveled the United States. He is also a professional photographer and author.

Q. What is the Foundation for Deep Ecology and why did it get behind the publishing project, *Thrillcraft: The Environmental Consequences of Motorized Recreation*?

A. The Foundation for Deep Ecology attempts to look beyond the obvious proximate causes for environmental problems, and looks at the ultimate systemic causes for environmental problems. Thrillcraft is the use of machines for speed and often-destructive behavior. As such it is systematic of a deep disconnect whereby people abuse the land and disturb other people who are seeking to enjoy the public property.

Q. How much damage are "thrillcraft," such as ATVs, doing to public lands in America? Is that damage as permanent as a chemical spill or a nuclear accident?

A. The damage is more like the impact of secondhand smoke. It may seem benign but over time the effects are significant. Nuclear accidents are concentrated. Thrillcraft affect more land over a larger area. The cumulative impacts occur on millions of acres together.

Q. ATV users argue that they enjoy the outdoors as much as any environmentalist, and they have as much right to enjoy their recreation form as any hikers or birders. Do they have a point?

A. I won't try to say whether they enjoy the outdoors or not. The fact is that their presence destroys the outdoors experience for others. Again, it's like smoking. Smokers can enjoy cigarettes in their home. But they impose their smoking on others in public places. We limit their "right" to pollute the public air.

Q. Critics of ATVs argue that Missouri can pass all the laws it wants, but there is not enough personnel to enforce the restrictions and nobody pays attention to them. Is that a valid criticism and is it a national phenomenon?

A. In a sense, that is why ATV use should be banned on public lands. ATV users are not responsible. The vast majority of them in surveys consistently say they violate the laws. Would we allow someone who consistently drove 50 mph in a 25 mph zone to continue driving? Or would we take away their "right" to drive?

Notes

1. Midwest Trail Riders Association, www.ridemtra.com.
2. Norbeck Society, www.norbecksociety.com.
3. Ibid.
4. National Statistics, www.atvsafety.gov.
5. Missouri Model Traffic Ordinance Section 300.348, www.atvsafety.gov/legislation/Missourilaw.pdf.
6. Wuerther, George, *Thrillcraft: The Environmental Consequences of Motorized Recreation* (Vermont: Chelsea Green Publishing, 2007).

Additional Readings

Devall, Bill, and George Sessions, *Deep Ecology: Living as if Nature Mattered* (Layton, Utah: Gibbs M. Smith, 1985).
Leopold, Aldo, *A Sand Country Almanac* (New York: Oxford University Press, 1949).
Martin, Calvin Luther, *In the Spirit of the Earth* (Baltimore: The Johns Hopkins University Press, 1992).
Wilkinson, Todd, *Science Under Siege* (Boulder, Colo.: Johnson Press, 1998).

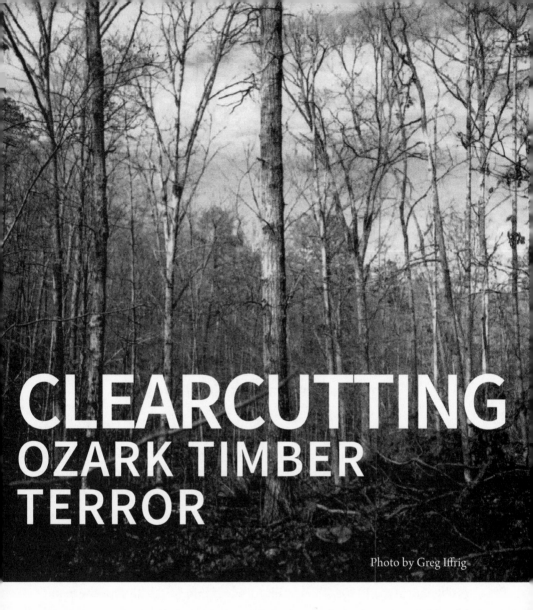

Photo by Greg Iffrig

CLEARCUTTING
OZARK TIMBER
TERROR

C learcutting has been a dirty word among nature lovers and environmentalists in Missouri for many years. That's because the wholesale destruction of forest cover in Missouri during the logging era did untold damage to Ozark rocky ridges and slopes, to animal habitat and adjacent farmland, as well as to once clear and pristine streams. Clearcutting is a controversial practice in which whole sections of forest are universally cut down and the timber harvested.

Massive clearcutting took place in southern Missouri from about 1880 to 1920. Lumber companies floated tons of downed timber, cut poles, and railroad ties down Ozark streams to railroad heads for transportation elsewhere.[1] Destruction of forests led to terrible soil erosion problems and the wholesale depletion of many wildlife species.[2] Clearcutting also meant a loss of natural resources that provided sustenance for residents of the area, who benefitted from jobs once provided by the timber industry.

By the 1930s, the state was overdue for action by the Missouri Conservation Commission, as well as ready for new forestry management practices. The University of Missouri established a Department of Forestry in its College of Agriculture, which encouraged more enlightened land use.[3] Nevertheless, it took years for some forests to recover, while other areas were permanently deforested and left for subsistence farming and cattle grazing.

Environmentalists Get Involved

In recent decades, environmental groups such as the Missouri Coalition for the Environment and state chapters of the Sierra Club have taken a keen interest in preventing clearcutting practices. However, it is difficult to restrict what happens on private property. Numerous instances can be cited in which cheap land is purchased or leased solely to clearcut timber for firewood for an easy buck.

Another concern regarding abuse of forest lands has been the harvesting of timber for the chip mill industry in the state. Woodchip mills began to proliferate in the 1990s. These mills turn logs into woodchips for the manufacture of particle board, paper, rayon, and other products.[4] A single large chip mill can process wood from more than one hundred acres of clearcut forest land per day.[5]

In his book, *The Ozarks: Land and Life*, Milton D. Rafferty describes the organization of the chip mill industry as resembling the sharecropper system of the old South. He also notes concerns "about the impact of removal of all forest cover, namely, soil erosion and the increase in soil load in streams, along with related deterioration of water quality and damage to aquatic life."[6]

A New Way: Single-Tree Harvesting

A successful forest management system as an alternative to clearcutting for timber was developed by Ozark landowner Leo Drey in the 1950s. His conservation ethic includes "watchful fire control and selective cutting," rather than wholesale clearcutting.[7] Drey also founded the L-A-D Foundation, which has refined techniques for uneven-aged forest management allowing for the retention of forest on every acre, even in the immediate aftermath of a harvest.[8]

The L-A-D Foundation continues to develop good forest management practices at Pioneer Forest in the heart of the Missouri Ozarks. Forest inventory data show that managing a forest by single-tree selection can be successful from a business standpoint, as well as an environmental perspective. Pioneer personnel have eagerly taken visitors through the woods to see how the process works. To learn more about these practices, visit www.pioneerforest.com.

Clearcutting Q & A

Terry Cunningham is with L-A-D Foundation which encourages responsible forest management practices.

Q. When does clearcutting result in deforestation?

A. Deforestation results when the land is cleared of trees generally with the intention or result of not regenerating into a forest. Examples are: Clearing forestland for pasture or other uses. This can be done by bulldozers, herbicides, etc. Clearcutting can be used initially to clear the land and recoup some of the expenses by selling products with follow-up clearing with machines. This is not a forestry practice but a conversion of a forest to another land use.

Q. Wasn't much of the Bootheel of Missouri covered by large timber forests before the loggers came in with clearcutting?

A. Actually, most of the Bootheel was swamps with both the Black River and the St. Francis River draining into it. The land was drained in the 1920s by digging diversion channels and laying drain tiles. However, there were areas of timber with bottomland hardwoods. Big Oak Tree State Park is one such example, along the Mississippi. Most of these areas were cleared for agriculture.

Q. Advocates of clearcutting argue that there are good scientific, economic, and safety reasons for clearcutting. Are any of these criteria valid when it comes to clearcutting?

A. I believe that most of these reasons can be valid or true in specific situations. However, the question to me is not whether there are valid reasons to cut down trees in this way, as clearcutting can result in regenerating an oak, hickory, or even a pine forest. But there are too many negatives associated with the procedure and there is a viable alternative, Uneven-Aged Management. Examples of negatives with clearcutting are erosion, effects on invertebrates and soil microorganisms, effects on forest canopy interior bird populations, etc.

Q. What are some examples of loss of habitat because of clearcutting in Missouri? What species have been especially hit hard?

A. Clearcutting favors early successional species such as Scarlet Oak and trees in the Red Oak group, so I'm not too sure of its effect on forest diversity. It favors browsers like deer in their early stages but discriminates against forest interior birds and neo-tropical songbirds.

Q. Some timber companies argue that single tree selection is bad because it depletes the best of the trees, and this results in weaker trees reproducing over time, weakening forests. Is this true?

A. This is not single-tree selection, but high grading. If you choose to select the best trees, this is indeed what will happen; but it is not good forestry nor proper single-tree selection. Proper single-tree selection removes the worst trees and keeps the best trees and allows them to grow to their full potential.

Notes

1. Rafferty, Milton D., *The Ozarks: Land and Life* (Fayetteville: University of Arkansas Press, 2001), 178-179.
2. Ibid., 185.
3. Ibid., 185-186.
4. Ibid., 191.
5. Ibid., 192.
6. Ibid., 185-187.
7. Ibid., 190-191.
8. Stetzler, Hank, "Pioneer Forest: A Leader in Uneven-Aged Management," *Green Horizons* (Winter 2005): 1-3.

Additional Readings

Ellison, John, and Christopher Harris, *Beloved of the Sky* (Seattle: Broken Moon Press, 1993).
Fritz, Edward C., *Clearcutting: A Crime Against Nature* (Waco, Tex.: Eakin Press, 1989).
Gibson, Arrell M., *Wilderness Bonanza: The Tri-State District of Missouri, Kansas and Oklahoma* (Norman: University of Oklahoma Press, 1972).
Russell, Jesse, and Ronald Cohn, *Clearcutting* (New Delhi: Book On Demand Ltd., 2012).

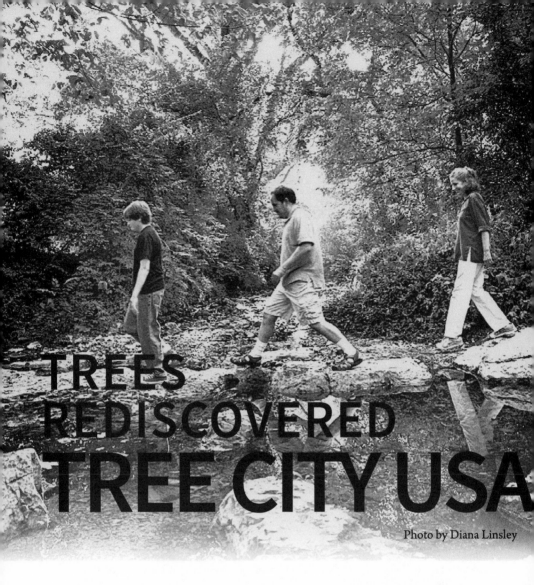

TREES REDISCOVERED TREE CITY USA

A t first just a few Missouri cities made the cut: Springfield, University City, Florissant, Des Peres, Parkville, Ellisville; but now more than seventy-five Missouri towns qualify as Tree City USA communities. Nationally, more than 3,400 communities are now classified as worthy of the Tree City USA designation.[1]

Although the fraternity of tree cities, sponsored by the Arbor Day Foundation in cooperation with the Forest Service, may not be as exclusive as it was a quarter-century ago, the distinction is still worth having. The title Tree City USA shows a community takes its trees seriously. Gone are the days when trees were simply mowed over to make room for a new tract of homes on a city's outer limits; gone are the days when trees were topped, scalped, denuded, and otherwise tortured to make sure city utility lines were unimpeded.

Leafy Webster Groves has been a Tree City USA town for three decades. Nearby Kirkwood has been a Tree City USA town for more than twenty years. They are legacy tree towns, but they have not been content to simply flaunt an accolade or to hype their positive public image and citizen pride from the highest treetop. The two towns have joined with nature and environmental groups to design citizen projects that save trees and promote awareness on how important, nay essential, trees are in our lives.

On the Hunt: For Trees

Stacy Arnold and Karla Wilson are unabashed tree huggers and well-known nature advocates in the St. Louis area. Arnold and Wilson were instrumental in establishing the great Webster-Kirkwood Mini Tree Hunt in the fall of 2011.[2] Twelve tree sites were selected as arboreal destinations to visit in order to successfully complete the hunt. Those who participated in the hunt had their tree identification journals validated by hunt organizers. Then they were entered into a drawing for a prize from a tree nursery.

However, the journey to find all the wonderful trees was the real prize for those who took up the challenge, according to Wilson, a Webster Groves resident. Tree totalers found themselves in the canopy of some great champion trees. Among them:

- A Kirkwood sugar maple tree, still thriving at age 250. The old-timer was dubbed a "Pioneer Tree" of distinction by the Kirkwood Urban Forestry Commission in 2003.

- A golden larch in Kirkwood planted in 1981 with seeds from the Missouri Botanical Garden. The seeds were from a tree that was a descendant of a tree given by China to the U.S. at the 1904 St. Louis World's Fair.

- The famous "Liberty Tree" in Larson Park in Webster Groves was a must on any tree hunter's list. The wide, sturdy, and much-weathered oak tree dates from the 1776 American Revolution and is in the gorgeous, riparian area of Shady Grove Creek.

Tree City USA projects, such as the great Webster-Kirkwood Mini Tree Hunt of 2011, help convert more residents into tree huggers. They come to realize that trees are not just naturally beneficial and aesthetically pleasing, they are downright cost-effective. Trees give us food; they prevent erosion and flooding; they add value to where they are located—they are cost-effective to have around.

Forest ReLeaf of Missouri

Mike Walsh, an ISA certified arborist and forestry programs manager with Forest ReLeaf of Missouri, can point to actual dollar figures that make the point that trees are cost-effective community attributes. He cites a study conducted by Forest ReLeaf that found tree canopy coverage in St. Louis provides a value to the city of $39.8 million.[3] More trees can mean less need for storm sewer construction necessary to handle storm surge. Planting more trees means less construction costs for storm water detention areas.

Then there are the environmental benefits of trees, Walsh notes. By absorbing and filtering out nitrogen dioxide (NO_2), sulfur dioxide (SO_2), ozone (O_3), carbon monoxide (CO), and particulate matter less than 10 microns (PM10) in size in their leaves, urban trees perform a vital air cleaning service that directly affects the well-being of urban dwellers. Studies by Purdue University have shown that trees remove pollutants in storm runoff as well—pollutants that include cadmium, chromium, copper, lead, nitrogen, zinc, phosphorous, and suspended solids.[4] Trees reduce the concentration of these pollutants entering our drinking water resources.

Trees Rediscovered Q & A

Mike Walsh is an International Society of Arboriculture (ISA)–certified arborist and forestry programs manager with Forest ReLeaf of Missouri. He also teaches tree-related classes at St. Louis Community College and Missouri Botanical Garden. He has worked for the MU Forestry Department and with the Missouri Department of Conservation, USDA Forest Service, and Horticulture and Agroforestry Research Center.

Q. What is a tree inventory and why should citizens insist that their communities take such inventories?

A. A tree inventory is a system of data collected about the trees in their community, mostly street and park trees. Data collection involves species, size (diameter at breast height), condition, maintenance needs (pruning, removal, etc.), site information (street tree, park tree, etc.), and other information such as the presence of insects or disease. Inventories are a valuable resource to any community. They let city foresters/arborists know vital information about the urban forest, which in turn helps them manage the urban forest. Tree inventories should be updated periodically to determine how the urban forest is changing over time.

Q. How do trees fit into the ecology of urban and suburban living?

A. Forests can intercept and slow rainfall, which allows more to infiltrate into the soil as opposed to running off into our rivers and streams. They sequester carbon in urban areas and provide much-needed oxygen and shade, which reduces the urban heat island effect. Even pockets of trees or a few trees in our urban lawns can benefit the community as a whole.

Q. Why do healthy, mature trees add value to the average residential property?

A. Deciduous trees can shade homes in the summer and allow sunlight to pass through in the winter to reduce heating and cooling costs. The National Arbor Day Foundation has found that trees can save up to 58 percent on home cooling costs in the summer with proper species selection and planting location.

Q. How could a concerted tree planting effort address the negative impact of our carbon footprint, and global warming?

A. Trees directly remove carbon from the atmosphere. In the city of St. Louis, CITYgreen Analysis has estimated that the urban forest sequesters 2,425 tons of carbon annually. If the urban tree canopy were to increase by 10 percent, that figure would rise to 3,371 tons annually.

Q. If a Missouri resident buys a new house on a suburban tract with no trees, what kind of a tree-planting program for the yard would be most practical to implement?

A. The best time to plant a tree was twenty years ago, and the next best time is now. My advice would be to research what sort of conditions are present at the home (soils, etc.) and speak with a local certified arborist or conservation department/ university extension office for more information. A planting and maintenance plan will insure a successful tree program. There are countless organizations dedicated to tree planting, and they can play a vital role in communicating proper tree planting practices to the public.

Notes

1. Arbor Day Foundation: 2012 Tree Cities USA Communities in Missouri, www.arborday.org/ programs/TreeCityUSA/treecities.cfm?chosenstate=missouri.
2. Corrigan, Don, "On the Hunt—For Trees," *Webster-Kirkwood Times* (September 23, 2011): 1.
3. Forest Releaf of Missouri: Urban Tree Canopy Assessment, www.moreleaf.org/pdfs/Stl%20 Urban%20Tree%20Canopy%20Assessment_final.pdf.
4. Purdue University Agricultural Research Studies, www.agriculture.purdue.edu/fnr/htirc/pdf/ news/purduehelpingtoremove.pdf.

Additional Readings

Collingwood, G.H., and Warren D. Bush, *Knowing Your Trees* (Washington, D.C.: American Forestry Association, 1974).
Davis, Beresford, and Diana Kroeger, *Arboretum America: A Philosophy of the Forest* (Ann Arbor: University of Michigan Press, 2003).
Little, Elbert L., *Trees* (New York: Alfred A. Knopf, 1980).
Pirone, P.P., *Tree Maintenance* (Oxford: Oxford University Press, 1988).
Rupp, Rebecca, *Red Oaks and Black Birches: The Science and Lore of Trees* (Vermont: Storey Communications, 1995).

H2O IN THE MO
WATER ISSUES

Photo credit Jill Moon/
Alton Telegraph

"Humans build houses on the land beside the sea, and the sea comes and takes them away. That is not land says the sea. . . . Humans keep busy dredging, filling, building, diking, draining the places between land and sea, trying to make them either one or the other."
—Donella H. Meadows
"Lines in the Mind," 1991

When MacArthur Fellow and Dartmouth Professor Donella Meadows writes in her nature essay about the land beside the water that is "not-sea, not-land," I have to smile. Places that are "not-land and not-river" can readily be found in the Missouri and Mississippi river valleys. My favorite encounter with this kind of place is biking the trails in the wetlands from the towering bluffs of Creve Coeur Park to the Missouri River.

In summer, this area can be parched, drought-stricken land as dry as that proverbial sun-drenched bone. In late fall and early spring, this same area can be "part-river," so filled with water from the heavens that it's time to call old Noah for help. Nevertheless, developers continue to covet this wetlands area for big box stores and other commercial encroachments.

Now, after development has destroyed so many wetlands in this country, we Americans are beginning to realize how valuable these spaces can be. And we want our wetlands back. Wetlands are vital for flood control, for cleansing water, for species preservation, and for playing an essential role in the balance of nature. Wetlands purify the waters of lakes and streams in ways that are superior to the contrivances of man. Quality, healthy water is a diminishing resource. The perils to clean water are many, from faulty sewer systems to industrial wastes and pollutants. This chapter takes a look at a number of environmental issues affecting our water resources. How sad that it's not uncommon these days to find neighborhood streams posted with warnings: "Do Not Play, Swim, or Fish." Beaches at state park lakes also have been posted with these kinds of "off-limits" warnings in recent years.

On a positive note, more and more Missouri residents are becoming involved in clean stream activities, demanding cleaner water and protesting the loss of wetlands. These are not trendy causes; these are matters of survival. As Meadows reminds us in her "Lines in the Mind" essay, we humans are mostly made of water: "When I drink, the water of the earth becomes me. . . . If the air and the waters and the soils are poisoned, I am poisoned."

POSTED
"NO PLAYING, FISHING, SWIMMING"

Photo by Diana Linsley

'll take all that sewage and pump her in the ground. We'll dump it in sinkholes and caverns all around."[1] These two lines from the late naturalist Roger W. Taylor's song, "Stinky Dinky Doo," can tell you all you need to know about the early history of the St. Louis sewer system. As St. Louis grew into a big city in the 1840s, outhouses were replaced by a system that pumped sewage into sinkholes and caverns, as well as into lakes and rivers.

All that sewage was "out of sight, out of mind," until seventeen inches of rain hit in June 1848 and the mess bubbled up from the ground and the ugly brew spilled out of creeks and lakes. A cholera epidemic followed that took the lives of about 6,000—about one in eleven citizens.[2] The disease loosened the bowels of victims who subsequently gushed what was known as ricewater stool (the floating white specks were pieces of small intestine lining).[3]

Obviously, all this raw sewage finding its way into sinkholes, streams, and rivers made for bad news in the 1840s—and bad news still today. In the summer of 2007, residents across the St. Louis region were alarmed to find creeks and streams in their neighborhoods posted with warning signs: "No Playing, Fishing, Swimming."[4] The signs were posted by the Metropolitan Sewer District (MSD) at the behest of the Environmental Protection Agency (EPA). The problem was sewer water and E. coli bacteria finding its way into the region's waterways. The source of the contamination was sewage overflows—untreated sewage flowing into storm water venues, streams, and creeks.

Back to Clean Water Act

"This problem goes all the way back to the 1972 Clean Water Act," explained Kathleen Henry, who is president of the Great Rivers Environmental Law Center in St. Louis. "The EPA made sewer overflows illegal in 1972. The EPA suggested that the MSD system should come into compliance by mid-1983. That never happened. This is a decades-old problem. You can only assume that it would have cost a lot less to fix the situation back in the 1970s, than it is going to cost now in a new century."[5]

The problem of sanitary sewer overflows (SSOs) is not unique to St. Louis. The EPA has estimated that upgrading every city treatment and collection system across the country to reduce the frequency of overflow events would be more than $88 billion.[6] The primary cause of SSOs is heavy rainfall, which causes water to overwhelm the storm water and sewage lines. The combined flow exceeds the capacity of sewer systems with the result that sewage overflows into streams and sometimes floods streets, homes, and businesses.

Sanitary sewer overflows are a worldwide problem. In the developed world, cities such as London, Paris, and New York struggle with antiquated systems that contaminate waterways. In the so-called underdeveloped world, the discharge of raw sewage into the environment is massive—thousands of times that of modern, industrialized countries. The results are not simply gastrointestinal illnesses, but chronic diarrhea and high rates of mortality.[7]

Legal Settlement with EPA

After a 2011 legal settlement with the EPA on the SSO problem, which requires MSD to spend several billion dollars to fix the sewer and storm water system issues, public hearings were held to discuss the contamination and its sources. MSD and Missouri's Department of Natural Resources (DNR) said it would take time and energy just to locate all the overflow points and origins of bacteria spills.

Lorin Crandall, clean water program director for the Missouri Coalition for the Environment, said that during the period in which careful study and mapping of water problems takes place, less-expensive strategies can be implemented for remediation. Rain barrels, rain gardens, tree plantings, and more can intercept rainfall and reduce the contamination from SSOs. He lamented that the St. Louis area may never have pristine streams again, "but they can be a lot better than they are."[8]

Wastewater and MSD Q & A

Kathleen Logan Smith is the executive director for Missouri Coalition for the Environment. The citizen organization aims to protect and repair the environment through education and legal action.

Q. St. Louis has a history of problems with its sewage. Is St. Louis any worse than other cities in this regard?

A. Many other cities in America took advantage of federal grants that helped pay the cost of upgrading sewers in the 1970s and 1980s. Not St. Louis. Part of our problem is ninety-two municipalities and numerous sewer systems that were cobbled together with the thin glue of government in the 1950s.

Q. How is raw sewage a problem for our recreational areas all over Missouri? What are the symptoms of sickness from exposure for a child or a pet?

A. Untreated sewage harbors bacteria, pathogens, viruses, and parasites. It is a cause of illness globally on a massive scale. E. coli is just an indicator species, and if you find that you can bet your boots there are other nasties in water where sewage is present. Untreated sewage also contains (often) lots of ammonia, which can spur algae growth, cause hypoxia, and kill fish.

Q. As many as 300 sewer pipes in the MSD system have overflow flaps. Will they be eliminated now that MSD appears to be ready to do the job of complying with the EPA on the problem of sewage and storm water mixing in rainy periods?

A. There were more than 500 when we started. Those refer to sanitary sewer overflows, which are overflows built into the system as a "relief" valve of sorts to a system that has capacity restraints—so they dump in the streams. The consent decree calls for elimination of Sanitary Sewer Overflows. It will take twenty-three years before they are all eliminated, but the ones near schools, parks, and homes on our smaller streams are prioritized. A list of fifty will get done within the initial months of this long project.

Q. Statewide, how much of Missouri is still operating with septic tanks that also pollute streams, rivers, caves, and caverns? If city sewers are impractical for these areas, are there sustainable alternatives?

A. A well-maintained septic system in the right ground can be fine. An ignored one that was never installed right in the first place or in the right ground is a problem. We have plenty of both. It would be really nice if people could learn to live with composting toilets. Certain drinking water lakes in New York solved a big problem with this simple, effective technology.

Notes

1. Taylor, Roger W., *Born in the County* (St. Louis: Kestrel Productions Press, 1995), 55.
2. Ibid., 52-53.
3. Cooperman, Jeannette, "Take Care, and Don't Take the Cholera," *St. Louis Magazine* (July 2010): 50-53.
4. Corrigan, Don, "Warning: Do Not Play, Swim, or Fish," *Webster-Kirkwood Times*, 1A, 8A.
5. Ibid.
6. EPA Executive Summary, "Report to Congress: Impacts and Control of CSOs and SSOs," August 2004, cfpub.epa.gov/npdes/cso/cpolicy_report2004.cfm.
7. Spendilow, Monica, "Sanitary Sewer Overflow," *Impeller Magazine*, 2004.
8. Tomich, Jeffrey, "Cities, MSD Blast Missouri for Expensive Stream Clean-up Plans," *St. Louis Post-Dispatch* (September 12, 2012): A8.

Additional Readings

Grant, Nick, *Sewage Solutions: Answering the Call of Nature* (British Columbia: New Society Publishers, 2008).
Jenkins, Joseph C., *The Humanure Handbook* (Grove City, Penn.: Joseph Jenkins, Inc., 2005).
Praeger, Dave, *Poop Culture: How America Is Shaped by Its Grossest National Product* (Port Townsend, Wash.: Feral House, 2007).

BEWARE
THE "RIVER DESPAIR"

Photo by Diana Linsley

t's been called an open sewer, a polluted drainage ditch, and the "River Despair." Yet, when French priests came to the St. Louis area and settled on its banks in 1700, they found it to be a gentle, natural stream with an abundance of wildlife. Like so many small rivers in America's urban areas, the river became an erratically flowing cesspool.[1]

Today, drivers using Interstate 44 to cross from the county to the city over this St. Louis waterway usually pay little attention to it, unless it's brewing up a stench. So, what happened? Can urban streams such as the River des Peres ever be restored to a semblance of their former glory? Those are the kinds of questions being asked by members of the River des Peres Watershed Coalition. The coalition is chaired by Danelle Haake and meets regularly on issues involving the river, which flows on-again, off-again, through the heart of the St. Louis area.

"The River des Peres and its tributary streams compose one of the few remaining bits of urban landscape that connects all of us in the region," said Haake. "Water that falls on rooftops in Sunset Hills, Crestwood, and Ladue will join together in the River des Peres."[2] Also joining in the River des Peres with the water runoff are road salts, chemicals, sewage overflow, litter, and discarded rubbish. Haake said many residents don't care much because they see the river as just a concrete channel that drains urban messes along the boundary of city and county.

Urban Stream Syndrome

The stretch of pavement near Shrewsbury and to the south is not representative of the entire River des Peres. In many places, the river and its tributaries remain unpaved, unstraightened, and unencumbered. However, much of the river suffers what has come to be known in contemporary environmental parlance as "Urban Stream Syndrome." The syndrome is the result of city planners and engineers converting a natural stream into a storm water and sewage remover.

River des Peres has been altered several times. A nine-year project completed in 1933 involved extensive straightening, regrading, and paving of the river's bed and banks to address increasing problems with flooding. The drainage of the river and its watershed was reconfigured so that water could be moved as quickly as possible from land to river. It then empties its contents into the Mississippi, which flows into the Gulf.[3]

In doing this River des Peres redesign, the area's water table was lowered, the habitat and hydrology of the river were severely damaged, some of the river disappeared underground, and much of the river was left as a paved eyesore that some call the "River Despair."

Turning Despair into Hope

The River des Peres Watershed Coalition's Cindy Duhigg, one of its many growing number of members, finds enthusiasm for every aspect of the coalition's mission, from improving water quality and habitat to ending industrial and sewage pollution. She also takes comfort in finding more and more Missouri residents joining "Stream Teams" to clean up rivers and watersheds.

"I live in South City and I know people don't realize what a rich history the River des Peres has," said Duhigg. "If we can revitalize that river, I feel we can bring back our whole city and be proud. I don't ever expect the river to be completely clean again, but at least it doesn't have to be toxic. And I think we can make it aesthetically pleasing as a greenway and recreation area. Other cities have done it, why not us?"[4]

"River Despair" Q & A

Danelle Haake is the chair of the River des Peres Watershed Coalition in St. Louis. The coalition is a nonprofit that desires to protect and improve River des Peres.

Q. How is the river and its tributaries affected by runoff?

A. The River des Peres is a spring-fed stream. This means that the flow of the river should be supplied in the winter and spring by snowfall and rain, while groundwater from the many small springs should keep the river flowing in the summer and fall.

The flow of the River des Peres has been severely altered by the impervious surfaces in the watershed. The rainwater flows across the paved surfaces and into the storm water system, which pipes the water directly into nearby streams with no treatment to remove the pollutants it has picked up along the way. The lack of recharge to groundwater leaves the stream dry in the summer while the spring storms cause the river to flood frequently.

Q. How can we even begin to change the situation with development, runoff, and raging tributaries?

A. Unfortunately, there is no magic bullet. As a community, we have been slowly incorporating important steps into our laws, rules, and regulations. New developments and redevelopments require consideration of storm water impacts. Medium and large developments must include storm water retention basins. Several communities have adopted ordinances that require buildings to be set back from the streams.

Q. What are some specific actions that individuals can take to change the situation?

A. Individual homeowners can use rain barrels to capture water from their downspouts for later release once the storm has passed. They can create a rain garden that will capture some of the storm water in a shallow basin and allow the water to drain into the soil. For both homes and businesses, pervious pavement and green roofs are effective at absorbing rainwater before it adds to the storm water and stream flooding. Plant a tree, or (even better) don't cut down healthy, mature trees. Besides having vast root systems to help water reach the groundwater system, trees can absorb vast quantities of rainwater and release it back into the atmosphere.

Q. St. Louis doesn't exactly have a noted reputation for environmental renewal. Do you really expect River des Peres to one day become a natural waterway that can be enjoyed from lush, verdant banks?

A. The St. Louis area boasts the most dense concentration of Stream Teams. Also, when the voters were asked to decide where to put tax money that is designated for community improvement and revitalization, they wanted to spend the money on improving our streams. These funds led to the creation of the Great Rivers Greenway District. I expect that at least portions of the river will become an asset to the community that we will be able to enjoy, not only from the banks, but from in the water.

Notes

1. Corrigan, Don, "Restoring The River Des Peres," *Webster-Kirkwood Times* (April 18, 2008): 1A, 14A.
2. Ibid., 14A.
3. Allen, Michael R., "The Harnessed Channel: How the River Des Peres Became a Sewer," Preservation Research Office (November, 2010). See also: preservationresearch. com/2010/11/the-harnessed-channel-how-the-river-des-peres-became-a-sewer/
4. Corrigan, 14A.

Additional Readings

Bullard, Loring, *Healing Waters: Missouri's Historic Mineral Springs and Spas* (Columbia: University of Missouri Press, 2004).

Canfield, Marsha, "Citizens Opposition Sinks Des Peres Plan," *St. Louis Globe-Democrat* (October 19, 1972).

Hurley, Andrew, *Common Fields: An Environmental History of St. Louis* (St. Louis: Missouri Historical Society Press, 1997).

Metropolitan Sewer District (MSD), *The River Des Peres . . . A St. Louis Landmark* (St. Louis: Metropolitan Sewer District, 1988).

USGS Fact Sheet, "Effects of Urban Development on Floods," pubs.usgs.gov/fs/fs07603/.

USGS Water Science for Schools Resource, ga.water.usgs.gov/edu/impervious.html.

MERAMEC
MISSION
OPERATION
CLEAN STREAM

The modern environmental movement can be traced to any number of events: the publication of Rachel Carson's *Silent Spring* in the 1950s; the launch of the sloop *Clearwater* as a rallying point for the cleanup of the polluted Hudson River in New York in the 1960s; the celebration of the first Earth Day with environmental teach-ins across America in 1970.

In Missouri, two important events in the relatively short stretch of the state's environmental history have to be the launch of Operation Clean Stream in 1967 and several years of protest that led to the defeat of a proposed dam in eastern Missouri in 1978. Both of these events involve the Meramec River, a long, winding waterway that extends some 228 miles across the eastern portion of the state.

It's no wonder many Missourians favored damming the good-for-nothing river and creating a Lake of the Ozarks recreation area closer to the population center of St. Louis. The Meramec was a sick and polluted river in the 1960s—a natural disaster. Its condition inspired an initial group of about one hundred people to organize the first conservation cleanup of the river.[1] That cleanup became known as Operation Clean Stream. According to the early founders, the cleanup was actually modeled after the Clearwater project in New York, which was itself named for the song by Pete Seeger, "Clearwater." The original Meramec cleanup spawned similar events in the St. Louis region and Missouri, and also provided the nucleus for a local environmental movement to stop the Meramec Basin Project.

Dodging a Bullet, Dodging a Dam

The Meramec River begins in the Ozark highlands area of mid-Missouri and grows in size as it flows past forests, bluffs, and springs to empty into the Mississippi River below St. Louis. European settlers and their descendants were not kind to the river, as it became a mere shipping route for lead, iron, timber, and in later years, sand and gravel. Abused and unruly, the river was slated for a makeover in the 1960s. The U.S. Corps of Engineers planned to dam the river for flood control and to create a huge recreational lake southeast of Sullivan about a ninety-minute drive from St. Louis.

Corps' plans for the river hit a snag when environmentalists said "no" to a Meramec dam. They did not want the kinds of noise, traffic, pollution, honky-tonk shops, and outboard motors and their wakes that came with the Bagnall Dam on the Osage River on the other side of the state. They argued that the Meramec offered plenty of recreation for boaters, anglers, and swimmers as a free-flowing river. A giant lake was not wanted.

Environmentalists organized grassroots opposition that was successful in getting a referendum on the project for the affected counties. In August of 1978, almost 65 percent of state voters rejected the dam proposal.[2] Construction was stopped, and President Jimmy Carter defunded the project that would have permanently changed the landscape and topography of hundreds of square miles of Missouri.

Operation Clean Stream Continues

Today, the upper Meramec supports diverse flora and fauna, and fish populations ranging from crappie, catfish, and bass to trout and mussels. The lower Meramec near St. Louis still has problems, but its health is gradually improving. In 2012, Operation Clean Stream celebrated its forty-fifth consecutive annual cleanup with nearly 2,500 participants.

Stream volunteers cleaned up shores, shallows, and the waters' depths in hip boots, in scuba gear, and by canoe. Almost 35,000 pounds of discarded metal was retrieved, as well as 3,500 tires. In all, more than 440 cubic yards of trash was gathered in the two-day event, which is now a St. Louis–area environmental tradition.[3]

Clean Streams Q & A

Ron Coleman is the executive director at Open Spaces STL and has worked with its annual Operation Clean Stream (OCS) project. The project organizes volunteers to clean up the Meramec River and its tributaries.

Q. If the results of the 1978 referendum on damming the Meramec had been different and it was dammed, how would the Meramec Basin look today? What would be the environmental consequences?

A. Most all of the fish, forestry, and wildlife resources associated with the rivers and streams would have been greatly altered or totally eliminated from the planet. Due to the highly karst topography in the region a number of major caves would have been flooded and thousands of acres of habitat, forest cover, and fertile farmland lost.

Q. How much of an accomplishment is it that the Meramec is one of the longest (220 miles) undammed rivers in America today? Aren't dams being blown up and removed in some parts of the United States?

A. The Meramec River today is one of only seven free-flowing streams in the state of Missouri, allowing the river to function in a natural manner. Some rivers have also changed course over time and have silted in behind the man-made structures installed for various reasons. They were found to serve no real benefit and therefore removed.

Q. The Upper Meramec is so pristine compared to the Lower (urbanized) Meramec. Is there anything that can be done to address this inconsistency?

A. The water clarity changes to a more dingy color, reflecting the many impacts from dated agricultural practices, historic gravel extraction, loss of forest cover, and development pressures. The lower river, however, is much better today as a result of improved land use rules, storm water controls, and emerging greenway.

Q. Is it frustrating to see Operation Clean Stream pulling out tires, refrigerators, and bed springs year after year? Does this point to the need for stiffer dumping regulations in the state?

A. Well maybe, but we do have laws on the books, and things really are so much better in the watershed today. You must remember that OCS has been at work cleaning up a century or more of abuses. Many of the items collected show their age. Tires remain the biggest concern and we have been pondering ways to keep them out of our rivers, but again many of the tires picked up are also dated.

Q. There are a number of creeks draining watersheds into the Meramec, such as the Huzzah, Courtois, and Dry Fork. Do any of the creeks' sources drain toxics or sewage that calls for action upstream on these tributaries?

A. We believe that healthy tributaries are a key to a healthy Meramec River and Gulf of Mexico. Everyone lives downstream. The issues on the Upper Meramec and its tributaries are monitored pretty closely by the Missouri Department of Natural Resources, Missouri Department of Conservation (MDC), and the local jurisdictions. Livestock and Ag use, where it touches the rivers and streams, are the biggest concerns, but MDC is working closely with landowners to insure for good BMPs and good forest management practices.

Notes

1. Open Space Council, "Reflecting on the 45th Annual Operation Clean Stream," *Missouri Wildlife* (November 2012): 24.
2. Watkins, Conor, "The Meramec Basin Project: A Look Back 25 Years Later," www.rollanet. org/~conorw/cwome/article69&70combined.htm.
3. Open Space Council, op. cit., 4.

Additional Readings

Jackson, James P., *Passages of a Stream* (Columbia: University of Missouri Press, 1984).
McCandless, Perry, and William E. Foley, *Missouri Then and Now* (Columbia: University of Missouri Press, 2001).

E. COLI CLAMOR
LAKE OF THE OZARKS

F ans of actor Bill Murray will never forget his Baby Ruth pool scene from the movie classic *Caddyshack*. Contrary to Murray's smug declaration, it is a big deal when there's poop in the pool. Fecal material can spread bacteria like E. coli and Hepatitis A, as well as other parasites and germs. Everyone needs to get out of the water—whether it's a pool, river, or lake—when the presence of high levels of E. coli are detected.

E. coli contamination was a very big deal in May 2009 when water samples taken at public beaches at the Lake of the Ozarks revealed high levels of the bacteria's presence. Even though levels of E. coli at some locations were at eight times the maximum level considered safe, the Department of Natural Resources (DNR) chose not to reveal its findings for a month. There was concern that the release of the contamination information would put a crimp on Memorial Day tourism and hurt businesses around the lake.[1]

When the DNR's suppression of its findings came to light, there was a firestorm of criticism of the agency and of the administration of Missouri Governor Jay Nixon. Some in the state legislature called for an investigation and hammered away at Nixon for months. Eventually, the DNR had to admit a mistake in delaying release of its findings and in its denial of any danger to the public.[2] Also, the agency began publishing its monitoring efforts on a website for the public, and it began sending out numerous news media alerts on E. coli problem areas and beach closings.

Short- and Long-term Effects

Otherwise known as Escherichia coli, the rod-shaped bacterium E. coli is commonly found in the lower intestines of warm-blooded animals.[3] When the E. coli bacteria find their way into water, exposure can lead to infections of varying severity. The majority of those who pick up water-borne illnesses complain of nausea, stomach cramps, and diarrhea.

Some of those stricken with sickness from E. coli exposure may develop hemolytic uremic syndrome (HUS), which results when a toxin released by the bacteria damages blood vessels, often prompting kidney failure, gastrointestinal complications, and neurological issues.[4] Long-term effects can include heightened risk of kidney disorders, cardiovascular disease, heart attack, and stroke.

Sources of Contamination

A variety of sources for E. coli contamination exist, including leaking septic tanks and sewage systems, faulty wastewater treatment, tainted run-off, and illegal dumping. Environmentalist Ken Midkiff argues that cracking down on owners of leaking septic tanks and sewage systems is only a short-term pollution solution. Midkiff told the *Columbia Missourian* that the long-term solution to E. coli contamination is for the state legislature to provide better funding of the Department of Natural Resources (DNR) to monitor state waterways and to identify the polluters. "The DNR is vastly underfunded and understaffed. . . . The fault for much of the failure to monitor and enforce water quality laws lies with the state legislature."[5]

The problem of unhealthy water is not isolated to the Lake of the Ozarks. As the *Riverfront Times* of St. Louis noted in its coverage of the lake scandal, many stretches of Missouri's 155,000 miles of streams often have far higher levels of contamination. "People are floating, boating, fishing, and swimming in some of those waterways right now, downstream from a municipal water-treatment facility or a large factory farm with an unchecked spillover from a lagoon of animal waste (two major sources of elevated bacteria counts)."[6]

E. coli Contamination Q & A

Ken Midkiff is the chair of the Conservation Committee of the Osage Group Sierra Club in Missouri.

Q. The problem of E. coli contamination affecting lake and river activities hit Missouri newspapers in 2009—and Governor Nixon's administration was taking a hit for it. In reality, how long has this been a problem in the state?

A. E. coli contamination was not causing major problems until about 1982. It should be noted that E. coli can be found normally in mammalian innards, the problem is when it gets into the environment. Most bacterial contamination issues are based on the amount of E. coli that has, for example, gotten into water habitats. That is bad in itself and is an indicator of other bacteria. There is evidence that it may have been a problem since 1982, but the first indication I can find of "bacterial contamination" was in 1996, while David Shorr was DNR director.

Q. Some areas of Lake of the Ozarks have been tested at 2,400 colonies of E. coli per 100 milliliters, and creeks in St. Louis County have tested at 20,000 colonies per 100 milliliters. How does this affect waders or swimmers at these levels? Are you okay if you don't swallow?

A. Ingestion is most harmful, sometimes fatal. If there is any "opening" on the skin, such as abrasions or a laceration, bacteria enters. This usually results in infections, and sometimes in mild, flu-like symptoms. Some people are apparently quite sensitive to E. coli; others seem to be immune.

Q. Are there water clarity testers in my neighborhood? What would it take to enlist state citizens to be volunteer E. coli testers? Isn't the Lake of the Ozarks Watershed Alliance (LOWA) doing something like this?

A. Stream Team members (such as me) are not taught to do tests for bacteria, but most universities have a lab that will do such tests. At MU, all I need to do is submit a quart or so of water. Due to "chain of custody" issues, this cannot be used as evidence in a court of law. LOWA has a grant from DNR (via AmerenUE) to collect samples, but actual testing is done in the DNR lab.

Q. The Jacks Fork and Current rivers have had some distressing results with E. coli testing in the past. Have there been any restrictions put on sewage, dumping, or trail riding as a result?

A. There have been some restrictions placed on sewage treatment facilities at private campgrounds (Circle B in Eminence is one such) and on some public facilities operated by the City of Eminence. There are various proposals, yet to be enacted, to limit horse trail crossings on the Jacks Fork. By the way, after several studies and the concerns raised, stretches of the river still do not meet Water Quality Standards for high levels of bacteria. DNA tests show that most of the E. coli is from horse poop.

Notes

1. Miller, Amanda, "E. Coli at the Lake of the Ozarks: One Year Later," *Columbia Missourian*, www.voxmagazine.com/stories/2010/05/13/e-coli-scare-lake-ozarks, 1.
2. Ibid., 3.
3. CDC National Center for Emerging and Zoonotic Infectious Diseases, www.cdc.gov/ecoli/index.html.
4. Ubelacker, Sheryl, "E. Coli Infection," www.huffingtonpost.ca/2012/10/09/e-coli-infection_n_1952828.html.
5. Miller, 4.
6. Pflaum, Nadia, "Missouri's E. coli Problems Are Not Confined to the Lake of the Ozarks," *RFT* (July 16, 2010), 1.

Additional Readings

Ferrey, Steven, *Environmental Law: Examples & Explanations* (New York: Aspen Publishers, 2009).
Fiorino, Daniel J., *The New Environmental Regulation* (Cambridge: The MIT Press, 2006).
Hilgenkamp, Kathryn, *Environmental Health: Ecological Perspectives* (Sudbury, Mass.: Jones & Bartlett Publishers, 2005).

ASIAN CARP
MISSISSIPPI
INVASIVES

Photo credit Jill Moon/
The Telegraph, Alton, IL

I f you are looking for a good fish story, you can hardly do better than seeking out tales of the Asian carp. News stories on the Internet harp on the carp and complain about the "Asian Invasion." These fish stories may also contain imbeds that direct you to YouTube sites declaring "Flying Fish, Great Dish." A story distributed by *McClatchy-Tribune Information Services* notes the threat to native fish from the Asian carp, then borrows a line from the ancient Greek Horace with its conclusion: "Carpe carp," as in "Seize the carp."

It may be too late to seize the carp. The alien carp invasion is becoming a thorough and overwhelming American environmental problem. The huge fish, more appropriately referred to as silverfins, are working their way up the Mississippi and Illinois rivers and are a threat to the multibillion-dollar, commercial fishing industry of the Great Lakes.[1] They are voracious eaters; they crowd out and overwhelm native species; they have no natural enemies—no known predators who might reduce their expanding populations.

During the 1970s, silverfin and bighead were imported into the United States for use in commercial catfish ponds to clean the algae. They also were brought in with the approval of the Environmental Protection Agency (EPA) to be eco-friendly cleaners of sewage treatment lagoons. Within a decade, the carp escaped confinement in ponds during flooding and entered the waters of the Mississippi River basin and other large rivers.[2]

Disturbing the Ecology

Today, Asian carp thrive in twenty-three states. Their mind-boggling population growth is disrupting the ecology of rivers in the Midwest, including the Missouri, Illinois, and Mississippi. The fish can grow to one hundred pounds or more. Asian carp may now account for 60 percent of the total fish biomass in the Illinois River, according to a study released by Southern Illinois University at Carbondale.[3]

Asian carp differ from common carp, catfish, and buffalo, because they are not bottom feeders. They eat solids, plankton, and algae at the surface of the water. The feeding behavior accounts for the low level of chemical contaminants found in their flesh when compared to their bottom-feeding cousins.[4] Also, their tendency to be at the water's surface contributes to their habit of jumping and "flying" out of the water when boats come by and disturb them.

Stories of large Asian carp jumping out of the water and slapping boaters in the face—even knocking them unconscious—are not uncommon. On the Missouri River, fishermen are known to protect themselves from Asian carp with barrier nets. Duane Chapman, a fish biologist with the U.S. Geological Survey, told Connect.Cleveland.com that the airborne carp can hit the throttle of a boat, "and that's dangerous. Someone could fall out and even be run over by his own boat. There are times when a fisherman doesn't come home, and who knows what happened out there on the river?"[5]

Making Lemons Out of Lemonade

While environmentalists fret about what these slimy invasives are doing to the ecology of North American waterways, Chef Philippe Parola of Louisiana argues that when you've got lemons in the lake—or river—make lemonade. When you've got Asian carp, harvest them by the ton for freshwater food in the United States—and also send as many as you can back to China to address the trade imbalance.

"Salut! Silverfin Craze welcomes you to our website," declares Parola on his Internet site at www.silverfincraze.com. "Our primary focus is the conservation of the United States inshore fisheries and environment by promoting under-utilized fish species. . . . As a professional chef, I can ensure that all varieties of freshwater carp are excellent quality fish—including the now famous Asian carp, also known as silverfin."[6]

Asian Carp Q & A

Roy Brabham is with the Silverfin Marketing Group and works with Chef Philippe Parola on his Asian Carp project. Parola is attempting to create a consumer market for invasive species like Asian carp.

Q. You seem to feel that wild fish can actually be better than farm-raised fish for a variety of reasons. Can you explain some of those reasons?

A. Some would argue that farm-raised fish like catfish and tilapia avoid the food chain accumulation of toxic substances, but this is not necessarily the case, as such farmed fish are typically fed fish-meal derived from fish that are subject to these kinds of contamination. Another problem with farmed fish lies in the fact that large numbers of these fish are crammed into ponds or pens. This is similar to the concentrated animal-feeding operations such as those used for chickens. These conditions promote growth of pathogens like bacteria, yeasts, and parasites, and significant amounts of antibiotics and pesticides are needed to avoid infection issues. Antibiotics accumulate in the fish flesh and are passed on to consumers.

Q. Why do carp, buffalo, and silverfin have such a nefarious reputation in America? You seem to make a good case that these are pretty "good-eating" fish. Explain how you make your case.

A. These fish are widely regarded as "trash fish," particularly the invasive varieties such as Asian carp. This immediately creates a negative image, one that is not necessarily deserved, as in the case of Asian carp. This is a very clean and tasty fish that is well regarded by people who can be convinced to try it. The name of a fish can also cause negative perceptions. This situation led us to brand our Asian carp value-added products as silverfin.

Q. Any recipes that you will be suggesting for the silverfin? Is it necessary to camouflage or to accent their taste for the American palate?

A. There are a number of recipes available at www.chefphilippe.com in the Asian carp subsection of the Invasive Species section. This is a very clean fish with a mild taste, so it is not necessary to camouflage the taste.

Q. How will environmentalists like your idea of harvesting and processing these fish?

A. Since we will only be removing fish that are presently disrupting ecosystems in a very extensive way, there should be no conflict with environmentalists. We will not be able to and are not seeking to eliminate Asian carp, but to remove enough to reduce their negative impact on local ecosystems. Perhaps through such efforts, we can reach an ecological balance such as exists in China, where these fish are native.

Notes

1. Vierebome, Peggy, "Potential Impact of Asian Carp Invasion's No Fish Story," *Madison (Indiana) Courier* (June 16, 2012): 1-2.
2. USGS Columbia Environmental Research Center: "Invasive Carp Research Program," www.cerc.usgs.gov/Branches.aspx?BranchId=40.
3. Crosby, Tim, Southern Illinois University–Carbondale (April 20, 2012), news.siu.edu/2012/04/042012tjc12029.html.
4. Ibid.
5. Kavanaugh, Lee Hill, "Asian Carp, the New Bullies of America's Inland Waterways, Are Crazy, High-flying Fish," *McClatchy-Tribune News Service* (September 1, 2010); see also www.cleveland.com/nation/index.ssf/2010/09/asian_carp_the_new_bullies_of.html.
6. Chef Philippe Parola, www.silverfincraze.com.

Additional Readings

Asian Carp subsection of Invasive Species, www.chefphilippe.com.
Chef Philippe Parola, www.asiancarpsolution.com
Maeda, Deborah, editor, *Troubled Waters: Asian Carp and the Great Lakes* (Hauppauge, N.Y.: Nova Science Publishers, 2011).
Somervill, Barbara, *Asian Carp: Animal Invaders* (Mankato, Minn.: Cherry Lake Publishing, 2008).

CREVE COEUR LAKE WETLANDS LAST STAND

Photo by Diana Linsley

Wetlands consist of land areas that are saturated with water—think sponges. In the Midwest, these wetland sponges often are seasonally wet and provide a unique ecosystem for life, both above and below water. In addition to providing necessary habitat for plants and animals, wetlands also have been recognized as incredible filtration systems for cleaning polluted water and as barriers to reduce flooding. Unfortunately, for too many years, wetlands were simply viewed as useless swamps to be drained for development.

Even with efforts to prevent wetlands loss in recent decades, almost half of the world's wetlands have been drained for economic activity.[1] In Missouri, the situation for wetlands is far worse. The state has lost about 85 to 90 percent of its wetlands. Most of those that remain are along river corridors in less-populated areas. Efforts are now underway to restore or reconstruct lost wetlands.

One of those restoration areas is in the Creve Coeur Lake area of west St. Louis County near the Missouri River. The goal is to restore the area to a functioning wetland. About 550 acres of spongy land near Creve Coeur Lake Memorial Park is targeted for renovation. When completed, pools throughout the project area will run about three feet deep. Natural trails will permit visitors to view a swampy restoration, according to Dennis Hogan, environmental resource specialist with St. Louis County Parks.[2]

And what will visitors see when hiking the miles of trails in the restoration area? Lily pads, cattails, and marsh grasses will gradually come to dominate the area. Water birds such as ducks and blue heron, migratory fowl, tall wading birds, deer, small reptiles, and amphibians should all find a home in the restored habitat.[3]

A Good Supply of Water

One of the primary wetlands elements that had been missing in the restoration was a source of actual surface water. According to Mitch Leachman, executive director of the St. Louis Audubon Society, years of construction of highways and levees had left the entire wetlands complex with just rainfall and highway runoff as sources of recharge. A mitigation project was completed in late 2011 and basically involved piping to get water into areas deprived of natural flows.

A major pipe was installed from Creve Coeur Creek. The pipe runs underneath a roadway and recharges a shallow pond, with further distribution to other pools. Water flow isn't constant and the wetlands can dry out, but as Audubon's Leachman noted, that situation just mimics the natural process for wetlands. Environmentalists obviously would prefer wetlands in their natural state, but if it is necessary for them to be re-invented because of urban encroachment, then so be it.

Sierra Club members and the Audubon Society have assisted in the restoration of the wetlands. Their volunteers have picked up tons of trash and have planted trees and native vegetation.

Wetlands: An Important Bird Area

The Creve Coeur site was selected as an IBA (Important Bird Area) by the Missouri Audubon Society, because it has proven to be a significant habitat for migratory and breeding marsh birds. "We are working to establish IBAs for three main reasons," explained Sue Gustafson of Audubon. "An IBA increases public awareness of prime habitat; it leads to better protection of the area against future development; it opens the area up for more funding for education projects and environmental protection."[4]

Gustafson said she was elated when the Parks Department took on the Creve Coeur wetlands project and asked for input from nature and conservation groups. "Parks departments are usually interested in active recreation areas," said Gustafson. "This is a passive recreation area—an area that is going to be an attraction and a natural oasis for St. Louis and Missouri."[5]

Wetlands Q & A

Mitch Leachman is the executive director of the St. Louis Audubon Society.

Q. Wetlands have been divided into many classifications such as marsh, shrub swamp, swamp, oxbow, slough, bottomland prairie, etc. Is the Creve Coeur wetlands area a combination of these?

A. Yes. An inventory completed by Dennis Hogan, STL County Parks, in 2009 included marsh wetland, shrub swamp wetland, successional bottomland woodland and prairie.

Q. How important are wetlands for bird migration? How is this manifest in Missouri?

A. Nearly one-quarter of all U.S. birds rely on freshwater wetlands, including more than fifty shorebird species, seventeen long-legged waders, and forty-four species of ducks, geese, and swans. Many more species visit wetland areas during migration or occasionally during their breeding season for food and/or rest. Wetland bird populations are well below historic levels, but management and conservation measures have contributed to increases of many wetland birds, especially hunted waterfowl.

Q. Is it a problem if a wetlands area stays dry over an extended period?

A. Perhaps. Wetlands naturally fluctuate in their water level. In general, it is healthy for a wetland to "dry out" every so often. Of course, if that was to extend beyond more than a season, it would be a serious problem for the wildlife dependent upon the habitat, saying nothing of the functions mentioned above that benefit people.

Q. How might climate change have an impact on wetlands in Missouri?

A. The last climate change predictions I read for Missouri included much hotter summers, but not necessarily drier ones (Union of Concerned Scientists report from July 2009). The higher temperatures could result in more frequent storm events that might even increase the average precipitation. This may not have any long-term effect on "local wildlife," but would be a serious concern for flood storage and overall water quality as the limited remaining wetlands would likely not be able to handle the storm volumes.

Q. Why do wetlands areas often seem to be targeted for commercial development? Aren't they prone to flooding like the Chesterfield Valley in 1993?

A. Because they are "easy targets." For generations, wetlands and marsh areas were called "swamps" (and frequently still are). The average citizen knows little about wetlands and largely sees them as sources for mosquitoes and other pests. Government and commercial interests treated them as wasted land, unable to be farmed, logged, mined, or support the construction of homes/towns. From the 1800s (or even earlier), the country has systematically filled wetlands to create more "productive" ventures. Awareness of their wildlife value began in earnest at the start of the twentieth century, which resulted in protection of limited areas.

Notes

1. Handley, Thomas, "World Has Lost Half of Its Wetlands," November 29, 2012, news.mongabay.com/2012/1129-handley-wetlands.html.
2. Jackson, Harry, "Restoration of Wetlands Offsets St. Louis County Roadwork," *St. Louis Post-Dispatch*, A6.
3. Ibid., A1.
4. Corrigan, Don, "Birds of a Feather," *Webster-Kirkwood Times* (July 23, 2004): 1, 10.
5. Ibid., 10.

Additional Readings

Batzer, Darold P., and Andrew H. Baldwin, *Wetland Habitats of North America: Ecology and Conservation Concerns* (Berkeley: University of California Press, 2012).
Keddy, Paul, *Wetland Ecology: Principles and Conservation* (Boston: Cambridge University Press, 2010).
Mitsch, William J., and James G. Gosselink, *Wetlands* (New York: Wiley Press, 2007).

ENDANGERED

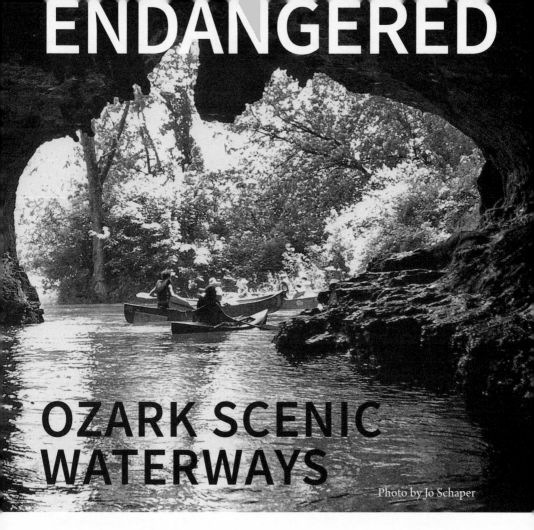

OZARK SCENIC WATERWAYS

Photo by Jo Schaper

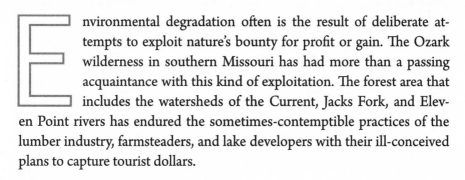

Environmental degradation often is the result of deliberate attempts to exploit nature's bounty for profit or gain. The Ozark wilderness in southern Missouri has had more than a passing acquaintance with this kind of exploitation. The forest area that includes the watersheds of the Current, Jacks Fork, and Eleven Point rivers has endured the sometimes-contemptible practices of the lumber industry, farmsteaders, and lake developers with their ill-conceived plans to capture tourist dollars.

First, there were the late-nineteenth-century timber operations that stripped river hills bare and removed the tree canopy which protected creeks and rivers from erosion. Farmsteaders allowed their stock to roam free through woods and streams, compacting soil and destroying wildlife habitat. Wide-eyed developers came along with schemes to dam the rivers and dot new artificial shorelines with ramshackle huts, faux cabins, and honky-tonk hotels.[1]

The beautiful area of rolling waters, tall limestone bluffs, and recovering forest clearly needed protection. In 1961, U.S. Interior Secretary Stewart Udall journeyed to the Current River to assess whether it made sense to include the region as part of the national parks system. Despite some hostile reaction from a few of the Ozark's locals to his visit, Udall was impressed and soon invited others from Congress to inspect Missouri's premier natural resource.

More information-gathering tours, negotiations, and legislative proposals eventually culminated in federal action to preserve for the first time an American river system.[2] On August 27, 1964, President Lyndon B. Johnson signed into being the Ozark National Scenic Riverways that gave federal oversight and protection to pristine areas of the Jacks Fork and Current rivers.

Waterways: Loved to Death

Initially, the vision for the new national park was to establish thirteen principal public access points. These would be about fifteen to twenty miles apart and configured to provide uninterrupted, day-long float experiences. Twenty years after President Johnson signed the riverways bill, thirteen developed river access points and public parks were in place. In the following three decades, however, use and abuse of the riverways began to spin out of control so that by 2011, there were more than 130 vehicular river access areas.[3]

Whereas the Ozark land and waters were once in danger of being exploited for mercenary reasons, now they were in danger of being "loved to death" by visitors with a multitude of recreational pursuits.

Environmentalists called on the National Park Service to do a better job balancing access and recreational activities with the need to safeguard basic river health and natural beauty.

Top Ten Endangered Riverways

The national environmental group American Rivers named the Ozark National Scenic Riverways to its "Ten Most Endangered Riverways in America."[4] Critics of American Rivers' report contend that Ozark streams do not belong in the same league with rivers suffering from natural gas "fracking," coal mining, sewage, and toxic spills. At a press conference in Kirkwood in May 2011, American Rivers and several other environmental groups pointed out why the Ozark Waterways were endangered:

- *Illegal Vehicular Use:* Motorized units from ATVs to heavy, off-road vehicles are causing bank erosion and damage to stream beds.

- *Scenic Easement Violations:* Homes, club houses, and recreation units are being sited on banks and bluffs that were supposed to be protected for scenic value.

- *Uncontrolled Equestrian Use:* Horse trails have proliferated along and through rivers, compacting soil along banks, and introducing bacterial pathogens into swimming areas from horse droppings.

- *River Congestion:* On summer weekends, stretches of river are jammed with canoes full of beer, boom boxes, and occupants exhibiting offensive behavior.

The National Park Service promised not to ignore the complaints but resolved to draft a plan to address them. In fact, several plans are under consideration.

Waterways Q & A

Greg Iffrig is a manager at the L-A-D Foundation, which aims to protect natural areas in Missouri.

Q. American Rivers put the Ozark Riverways on the Top 10 Endangered List in the U.S. How do you respond to skeptics who say there are far more endangered rivers because of coal mining, fracking, toxic spills, and more?

A. American Rivers is a national conservation organization working with citizens across the country seeking to make a difference for our rivers, and its in-depth review of conditions on the Current River compared with other rivers in America confirmed the seriousness of the problems. Regular sampling of river water indicates that its quality has been degraded (one of the characteristic native species inhabiting Ozark rivers, the hellbender salamander, has been disappearing from the Current River and now is listed as endangered).

Q. How do ATVS cause damage to streambeds and destruction of habitat for aquatic life?

A. Motorized vehicle intrusions at and along the river (including ATVs) contribute to unsettling the riverbed, sedimentation, and leaving behind gas and oil. One of the most dramatic responses to changes in the river is the continuing decline of the Ozark hellbender. Hellbenders were more commonly found in narrow reaches of the river where waters moved faster through large, irregularly shaped rocks. Now they seem more confined to less suitable larger pools.

Q. What are examples of scenic easement violations? Who is supposed to stop a club house or a dock from being built on the rivers? Do the locals view the rivers as theirs to do with what they want?

A. The intention of Congress was that this river be protected as a national park and always available and unimpaired for generations. In addition to fee title ownerships of parkland, there are more than 9,000 acres of privately owned land within the park boundary where NPS (National Park Service) officials purchased the right to limit certain future development in order to permanently maintain the scenic and natural integrity of the river's corridor. There seem to have been many violations. Photographs from river users show a number of larger buildings as well as new buildings within the riverways.

Q. Some canoe rental owners blame the political clout of horseback trail operations for why nothing gets done with the E. coli issues in the rivers. Are they shifting blame or are they spot on?

A. Pinpointing the problem is difficult since there may be multiple sources, including from septic tanks to the increasing level of commercial equestrian activities and consequently more than one approach may be necessary. State and federal officials must encourage work on a variety of solutions.

Notes

1. Kohler, Steve, *Two Ozark Rivers* (Columbia: University of Missouri Press, 1996), 95-96.
2. Ibid., 1.
3. American Rivers, "2011: Ozark National Scenic Riverways," www.americanrivers.org/endangeredrivers/2011-report/2011endangered-ozark.
4. Corrigan, Don, "Endangered Rivers: Ozark Rivers Threatened By Recreational Overuse," *Webster-Kirkwood Times* (June 3, 2011): 1, 12.

Additional Readings

Hall, Leonard, *Stars Upstream: Life Along an Ozark River* (Columbia: University of Missouri Press, 1969).

Nash, Roderick, *Wilderness and the American Mind* (New Haven: Yale University Press, 1981).

Tilden, Freeman, *The National Parks* (New York: Alfred A. Knopf, 1968).

Vance, Randolph, *We Always Lie to Strangers* (Westport, Conn.: Greenwood Press, 1951).

Photo by Diana Linsley

Section 3
CLEAN AIR
A RIGHT,
NOT A PRIVILEGE

"Certain inescapable facts are relevant ... more mouths to feed, a greater and greater demand for energy to run our industries and our homes, more digging for minerals and coal, more cutting of timber, more drilling for oil on- and off-shore, more automobiles to carry us around and foul the air. ... While we watched the horizon for mushroom clouds, a funnel-shaped one came up behind us with terrifying swiftness. It is perfectly clear now that we can destroy ourselves quite as completely, if not quite so spectacularly, through continuing abuse of our environment ..."
—Wallace Stegner
Marking the Sparrow's Fall, 1998

This section begins with a thick, gray smog and ends with the blue pall of wafting cigarette smoke. In between, we take a look at other air pollution issues such as ozone, airborne mercury, sulfur dioxide, and lead. However, the clean-air concerns involving smog and the pollutants from cigarettes offer a study in contrasts when it comes to how these issues have been handled in Missouri. To some extent, efforts to reduce smog constitute a success story. Efforts to reduce cigarette smoking have been less successful.

St. Louis was the smog capital of the world in the late 1930s and well into the 1940s. At times, the smog from burning coal was so bad that auto drivers could not navigate and planes couldn't land at the airport. The *St. Louis Post-Dispatch* did some of its best muckraking reporting when it took on the grit, the grime, and the coal industry. An organized smoke abatement movement was launched and dirty St. Louis cleaned up its act. Smog can still be a problem in St. Louis because of highway traffic and thermal inversions, but it is nowhere near the crisis proportions of the 1930s and 1940s.

Scientific studies have shown cigarette smoke to be every bit as hazardous to your health as the fumes and soot from thousands of chimneys belching exhaust from burning coal. Lung cancer deaths and fatal heart failures from smoking in Missouri number in the tens of thousands. It's not just the smokers who suffer, though. Studies show that secondhand smoke and even "thirdhand" smoke can be deadly. Nevertheless, efforts in Missouri to curb smoking and to tax cigarettes to fund smoking cessation programs have failed.

SMOG
GETS IN YOUR
EYES—AND LUNGS

Photo courtesy *St. Louis Post-Dispatch*

S t. Louis was once the land of the "midnight noons." Coal smoke filled the skies and crept along the ground. Smog was so thick that motorists had to turn their headlights on in the middle of the day.[1] This was particularly necessary in winters and cool months when coal furnaces were providing heat to homes and factories. Roads to the Gateway City had the distinction of leading into one of the most smog-polluted urban areas in the United States.

In 1926, the Citizens Smoke Abatement League estimated that the smoggy pollution was costing the city millions of dollars. The group noted that the annual soot deposit in the city was 870 tons per square mile, three times that of Pittsburgh.[2] The situation only worsened in the Depression years, and in November 1939 there were three solid weeks of dense smog.[3] The worst day occurred on November 28 and was dubbed "Black Tuesday." The haze lasted four days and city streetlights had to be lit in daytime hours.[4]

A Citizens Smoke Elimination Committee was formed and an anti-pollution editorial campaign hit the pages of city newspapers. A major problem was identified: The city was getting its energy and heating fuel from soft, dirty Illinois coal and needed to switch to cleaner anthracite coal. Politics and costs stood in the way of the switch to cleaner fuel, but eventually the transition was made. By the early 1950s, notable progress on smog was evident and the *St. Louis Post-Dispatch* cheered the triumph.

"A great city has washed its face, and its neck and ears, too," observed reporter Sam J. Shelton. "St. Louis is no longer the grimy old man of American municipalities. The plague of smoke and soot has been so well wiped off . . . the shining countenance is now the envy of other cities. . . ."[5]

New City Scourge: Photochemical Smog

Problems associated with smog don't simply involve grimy facades on buildings. Smog in St. Louis and other cities continues to present serious health issues. Some components of smog—carbon monoxide, sulfur dioxide, nitrogen dioxide, and ground-level ozone—are particularly harmful for seniors and children. Smog can cause eye, nose, and throat irritation; can interfere with immune functions of the body; and can cause emphysema, bronchitis, and asthma.[6]

Smog today is less from coal smoke and soot and more likely from vehicular traffic. Emissions from internal combustion engines, as well as industrial fumes, react in sunlight to form photochemical smog. The Environmental Protection Agency (EPA) Air Quality Index (AQI) lists current AQI data nationwide. Its site has basic information on smog and air quality, as well as links to other studies. The seminal May 2001 study titled "Fewer Cars Equal Fewer Asthma Exacerbations" details the link between automobile pollution and severe asthma.[7]

Smog Alert: St. Louis Worse Than Chicago

In late 2011, Environment Illinois released a report detailing how Chicago and St. Louis are among the most smog-ridden cities in the country. Despite Chicago's larger population and legendary traffic congestion, the report noted that St. Louis ranked seventh in smog pollution nationally, ahead of Chicago.[8] Bruce Ratain of Environment Illinois cited findings of physicians such as Dr. Susan Buchanan, director of the Great Lakes Center for Children's Environmental Health, who warned of increasing asthma attacks and fatalities.

At a press conference in St. Louis in late 2011, Ted Mathys of Environment Missouri and Dr. Gary Albers, pediatric pulmonologist and co-director of the Asthma Center, SSM Cardinal Glennon Children's Medical Center, issued similar warnings about smog. They lamented a push in Congress to roll back existing standards for smog pollution, rather than addressing a critical need for smog abatement efforts.[9]

Smog Q & A

Bruce Ratain is a clean energy associate for Environment Illinois.

Q. When smog dissipates with a cool front and accompanying rain, do the showers come down as noxious acid rain? What are the health effects of this phenomena?

A. According to the EPA, these health effects are indirect, and are caused when the NOx and SO$_2$ particles in acid rain accumulate in people's lungs. Scientific studies have identified a relationship between elevated levels of fine particles found in smog and increased illness and premature death from heart and lung disorders, including asthma and bronchitis.

Q. Where do NOx and VOx pollutants in smog come from?

A. NOx emissions come from the burning of fossil fuels in refineries, coal plants, and our transportation sector. VOx come from a variety of sources, including industrial facilities and transportation. Much of this pollution comes from "fugitive emissions" caused by leaks in refinery piping, etc., rather than just from the reported emissions coming from smokestacks.

Q. What is the pollution index or the American Air Quality Index? How are these measurements scaled and are they providing us with an index to smog and haze, or something different?

A. The American Air Quality Index, or AQI, measures levels of harmful air pollutants such as smog across the U.S., year-round. The AQI ranks air quality on a scale from 1–500 and announces "red alert" days when air quality is unhealthy, particularly for those most vulnerable (people with asthma, children, and the elderly).

Q. Some environmentalists feel it is time to establish an updated standard for smog pollution that is based on the most recent science. Is the EPA at work on this?

A. The current standard was set at a level that EPA's own board of independent scientists agree is not adequately protective of public health. The Obama administration considered updating the standard to protect public health, but the president decided in 2011 to abandon this effort until at least 2013.

Q. St. Louis is generally ranked in the Top 10 cities for smog. Can the city find a way to become more smog-free without changes in federal regulations?

A. Cities and states can do much to reduce our air pollution sources. Again, this pollution mostly comes from power plants, industrial sources, and cars—so policies to promote clean energy, more efficient and electric cars, and regulate industrial emissions can all help to curb smog.

Notes

1. Taylor, Roger W., *Born in the County* (St. Louis: Kestrel Productions Press, 1995), 66-67.
2. Ibid.
3. Ibid.
4. Ibid.
5. Neuzil, Mark, *The Environment and the Press* (Evanston: Northwestern University Press, 2008), 178.
6. "Who is most at risk from ozone?" www.airnow.gov.
7. EPA Air Quality Index site, www.airnow.gov, lists live AQI data nationwide.
8. "Study Finds Dangerous Levels of Smog in Chicago & St. Louis Areas," www.progressillinois.com.
9. "St. Louis Area Ranks Among Smoggiest in the Country," www.environmentmissouri.org.

Additional Readings

Devro, Davis, *When Smoke Ran Like Water: Tales of Environmental Deception and the Battle Against Pollution* (New York: Basic Books, 2003).
Kelly, William, *Smogtown: The Lung-Burning History of Pollution in Los Angeles* (New York: Overlook Hardcover, 2008).
Turko, Richard, *Earth Under Siege: From Air Pollution to Global Change* (New York: Oxford University Press, 2002).

OZONE
TWILIGHT
TOXIC ZONES

Photo courtesy of MoDOT

A mericans heard a lot about ozone in the presidential election of 2000. That's because Vice President Al Gore, the Democratic presidential candidate who won the popular vote, but lost the election, endured lots of derision and name-calling because of his environmental activism. Gore was called "Ozone Man," "Vice President Ozone," and "Senator Ozone" for his stands on global warming issues and more.

All that name-calling did have some beneficial effect in waking up Americans to what ozone is all about. Ozone in the upper atmosphere is a good thing, because it screens out large amounts of harmful ultraviolet radiation destined for Earth. Scientists became alarmed in the 1980s when they detected holes appearing in the ozone in the stratosphere. Leaders around the globe agreed to stop their countries from releasing chemical chlorofluorocarbons (CFCs) that were producing these dangerous holes in the ozone layer.[1]

Ozone at ground level is not as useful as what's up in the stratosphere. Ozone at ground level damages human health; it destroys plants and eco-systems upon which life depends; it also acts as a greenhouse gas, trapping heat and increasing the dangers of climate change.[2] Ozone is a pale blue gas with an odor much like chlorine bleach, and even low concentrations of ozone do damage to plastics, latex, and the lungs of humans.

Missouri Cement Kilns: Ozone Producers

Harmful molecules of ozone are formed by a chemical brew of ni-trogen oxides and organic compounds that "cook" in the sunlight. These pollutants can be sourced back to auto exhaust, gasoline vapors, power plants, factories, and cement kilns. Missouri is a virtual kiln capital with cement production factories that have been located over the years in cities such as Cape Girardeau, Festus, Hannibal, Clarksville, Sugar Creek, and more.[3]

Environmentalists have always been wary of the hazardous waste and gases produced by cement kilns, but in Missouri they became especially energized from 2001 to 2005 when Holcim (U.S.) Inc. sought permits for one of the largest plants in the world near Ste. Genevieve. Among groups fired up against the plant was the Webster Groves Nature Study Society (WGNSS). Because of the plant's location along the Mississippi River, WGNSS was alarmed by potential detrimental impacts to water quality, wetlands, and wildlife.

Perhaps even more distressing was the plant's threat to clean air. Estimates of regulated pollutants ranged up to 26,000 tons annually with 8,000 tons of the pollutants which form ozone.[4] A broad coalition of environmental groups fought the licensing and air permit for Holcim in Ste. Genevieve, stressing that the plant would harm any chance of the St. Louis region meeting federal limits on ozone pollution. In spite of the protests, Holcim prevailed, but the company was forced to make a number of design changes to reduce harmful emissions from the facility. The plant is the largest cement manufacturer in North America with 12,000 tons of cement produced per day.

Ozone Season of Summer 2012

For years, St. Louis and much of Missouri have failed to be in compliance with ozone limits set by the Environmental Protection Agency (EPA). Cement kilns are among the culprits in this failure. Inability to meet attainment levels can jeopardize federal highway funding, among other consequences. In the unprecedented heat, drought, and stagnant air of the summer of 2012, ozone concentrations skyrocketed.

Dr. Mary Castro, a pulmonologist and professor of medicine and pediatrics at Washington University School of Medicine, told the *St. Louis Post-Dispatch* about a spike in asthma, emphysema, and bronchitis cases. She said the connection between bad air and public health "doesn't just exist in scientific literature. Physicians see the effects directly."[5]

Ozone Q & A

Stuart P. Keating is an advocate for Environment Missouri.

Q. Pollution from automobiles causes ozone and in the summer results in ozone alerts. What are the various stages of ozone alerts and what agencies track the presence of ozone?

A. The Environmental Protection Agency issued a set of National Ambient Air Quality Standards in 1970, which list acceptable amounts of air pollution for six "criteria pollutants." Among the six criteria pollutants is ozone. Green is the lowest level of alert, using a scale of 0 to 50. Yellow is an intermediate alert, occurring when the AQI (Air Quality Index) is between 50 and 100. Orange is an elevated alert, meaning the air is unhealthy for sensitive individuals, such as the elderly, the very young, or those with asthma or respiratory illnesses. Red, predictably, is reserved for times when the air quality is dangerous to everybody.

Q. Ozone pollution in Missouri is not only caused by auto exhaust, but also by the state's cement kilns. What are these cement kilns and how do they contribute to ozone?

A. When a cement kiln heats limestone and clay to such high temperatures, many gases are released, including nitrogen oxides, sulfur dioxide, and a slew of volatile organic compounds. All of these gases combine to form ozone and smog. Additionally, the fuel used for these cement kilns often produces the precursor gases for ozone, in addition to other more toxic substances.

Q. How does industry located on the Mississippi River, such as cement kilns, result in higher ozone levels across the river in Illinois?

A. Air, water, and pollution do not respect political boundaries. Much of the land in Illinois and Missouri that surround the Mississippi River are low-lying floodplains. Air pollution produced on the Mississippi River can easily flow throughout these floodplains and indeed is often constrained within the floodplains by surrounding highlands and bluffs. Since the prevailing winds in the region are west-to-east, this means air pollution such as ozone from Missouri will flow right across the river into Illinois.

Q. The EPA has been considering lowering the levels for what is acceptable for ozone presence in the atmosphere. What is a permissible level of ozone?

A. Ideally, there would be no ground-level ozone, save for the ozone occasionally created by lightning strikes. The current standard for ozone is .075 PPM. Environment Missouri urges a further reduction, preferably to below .06 PPM.

Notes

1. "A Giant Sunshade," www.eco-action.org/dt/ozone.html.
2. Environment America: "Dirty Energy's Assault On Our Health: Ozone," environmentamerica. org/reports/ame/dirty-energys-assault-our-health-ozone.
3. Taylor, Roger W., *Born in the County* (St. Louis: Kestrel Productions Press, 1995), 99-100.
4. See Missouri Sierra Club: "Update On Proposed Holcim Cement Plant," missouri.sierraclub.org/ emg/sierrascape/s2003m12/01_update.html.
5. Tomich, Jeffrey, "A Breath of Stale Air Hangs Over the Area," *St. Louis-Post-Dispatch* (September 6, 2012), A1, A6.

Additional Readings

Alley, Richard B., *Earth: The Operators' Manual* (New York: W.W. Norton, 2011).
Benedick, Richard Elliot, *Ozone Diplomacy: New Directions in Safeguarding the Planet* (Boston: Harvard University Press, 1998).
Fishman, Jack, and Robert Kalish, *Global Alert: The Ozone Pollution Crisis* (New York: Plenum Publishing, 1990).
Parson, Edward A., *Protecting the Ozone Layer: Science and Strategy* (New York: Oxford University Press, 2003).

LEAD
NO INHALING
WHILE AIRBORNE

S t. Louis has its 630-foot Gateway Arch, and thirty-five miles to the south, Herculaneum has its 550-foot lead smelter smoke-stack. The so-called "leadbelt" of Southeast Missouri is dotted with a collection of smokestacks from smelter operations that date back more than a century. None of them compare to the giant tower that stands sentry over the river town—affectionately tagged as "Herky" by its residents.

Lead mining is a major part of Missouri's economic history, and the first mining camps established by the French preceded the Declaration of Independence.[1] Before the Civil War, an entrepreneur named Moses Austin introduced the reverbatory smelter in Herculaneum, which replaced the many primitive, small furnaces dotting the countryside. St. Joseph Lead Company found the Mississippi River site of Herculaneum to be ideal for a modernized smelter in 1892. The smelter at Herky was improved and enlarged several times before the location became the smelter of Doe Run Mining Company.[2]

For most of the twentieth century, the smelter provided tax money for the town and filled the wallets of Herculaneum's residents with cash from company paychecks. However, the smelter smokestacks also filled the air with particulate matter, and in 1975, heavy metal studies began showing elevated blood lead levels in Herculaneum's children—levels that would qualify as poisoning by a neurotoxin. Herky's residents had regarded the smelter as a sure bet for work for generations, but in the 1990s, some of them began filing lawsuits with claims of adverse health effects due to lead exposure.

Lead Poisoning: Missouri and Beyond

Brenda Browning, who grew up in Herculaneum, never considered that raising a family in a house a block away from the giant smelter might constitute a health hazard for her children. The lead smelter was just an old neighbor, and the smelly air from the plant was taken for granted as a necessary inconvenience.

"It was a nuisance, but growing up in Herky, you were told and believed that if you didn't work at the plant, there was no harm," Browning told the *St. Louis Post-Dispatch* in June of 2012.[3] When her kids came down with health problems, and tests showed elevated lead levels in their blood, the smelter became more than a nuisance. She was one of the first to sue her industrial neighbor in 1995, and she received a settlement in 2000.[4] Many more lawsuits for millions of dollars followed that initial suit by Browning.

In the spring of 2012, *USA Today* published the results of an exhaustive, fourteen-month investigation of lead contamination in America with headlines such as "Living in a Lead-Fallout Zone" and "Danger Hidden in the Yard." The investigative series invited readers to explore more than 230 old lead-factory sites nationwide at ghostfactories.usatoday.com. The series noted that "even trace amounts of lead—particles so tiny they're barely visible—are enough to cause irreversible health problems in kids who ingest or inhale them."[5]

Environmental Risks vs. Jobs & Paychecks

In 2010, Doe Run Company announced that it was closing the Herculaneum lead smelter at the end of 2013 and paying out millions of dollars to correct environmental violations. Some folks in Herky complained that environmentalists and lawyers had cost jobs and the financial wherewithal of their old city. Then came news that Doe Run was going to build a new smelter with state-of-the-art technology.

The new plant was going to use a smelter process that cut harmful emissions of lead and sulfur dioxide. It also would save two hundred jobs from the closing of the old smelter and add as many as fifty new ones.[6] Area environmentalists said the April 2011 announcement sounded encouraging, but also too good to be true. Apparently it was. In the summer of 2012, Doe Run announced that it was dropping plans to build the new $100 million lead processing plant.

Airborne Lead Q & A

Tom Kruzen works with several environmental groups, including Missouri Coalition for the Environment, Missouri Heartwood, the Mark Twain Forest Watchers, and the Scenic River Stream Team Association.

Q. What is lead?

A. Lead is an elemental heavy metal. It is extremely toxic to most life forms and is especially dangerous to nerve tissue and brain cells.

Q. What are the symptoms of lead poisoning among those in Missouri who have lived close to the lead mines or the smelters?

A. Peripheral nerves like the auditory nerve are often damaged, leading to hearing loss and numbness or tingling in the extremities. IQ loss is much more difficult to substantiate, but researchers are pinning down lead poisoning as affecting the judgment centers in the brain and especially the frontal lobe.

Q. Since lead was mined and smelted all the way back to the late 1700s in the state, could it be described as Missouri's number one toxic legacy?

A. It is America's number one toxic legacy. In the 1920s, it was widely used in gasoline as an anti-knock chemical, and before that it was used in paint to brighten the white and add hardness. It was known to be toxic in paint, and in 1897 the British paint company Apinalls advertised that they did *not* use toxic lead in their paint. At the same time American companies like National Lead and Glidden paint were busy using the image of the little Dutch Boy to sell lead paint as "healthy" for children.

Q. Don't tall smokestacks on plants like the "Herky" smelter go a long way in insuring that the pollutants are dispersed? Do the prevailing westerlies blow it across the river?

A. Tall smokestacks only disperse the toxic emissions. They do not render them harmless. This is a line of thinking that says that "dilution is the solution to pollution." Yes, the westerlies have blown lead emissions into the cornfields of Illinois.

Q. The lawsuits over airborne lead contamination are civil, but is there criminal negligence as awareness increased that lead is a neurotoxin?

A. Yes, the suits so far are civil but should be criminal. The Lead Industries Association made sure for eighty years that there was plenty of bad science and plenty of denial around to cloud any criminality. Proving criminality is difficult, and statutes of limitations are a problem.

Notes

1. Rafferty, Milton D., *The Ozarks: Land and Life* (Fayetteville: University of Arkansas Press, 2001), 126-127.
2. Ibid., 128-129.
3. Thorsen, Leah, "Lawsuits Pile Up Against Doe Run Lead Smelter," *St. Louis Post-Dispatch* (June 4, 2012): A1, A4.
4. Ibid., A4.
5. Eisler, Peter, and Alison Young, "Living in a Lead-Fallout Zone," *USA Today* (April 20, 2012): 1A.
6. Ibid., 6A.

Additional Readings

Denworth, Lydia, *Toxic Truth: A Scientist, a Doctor, and the Battle Over Lead* (Boston: Beacon Press, 2009).

Frank, Patricia, and Alice M. Ottoboni, *The Dose Makes the Poison: A Plain-Language Guide to Toxicology* (New York: Wiley, 2011).

Markowitz, Gerald, and David Rosner, *Deceit and Denial: The Deadly Politics of Industrial Pollution* (California: Milbank Books, 2003).

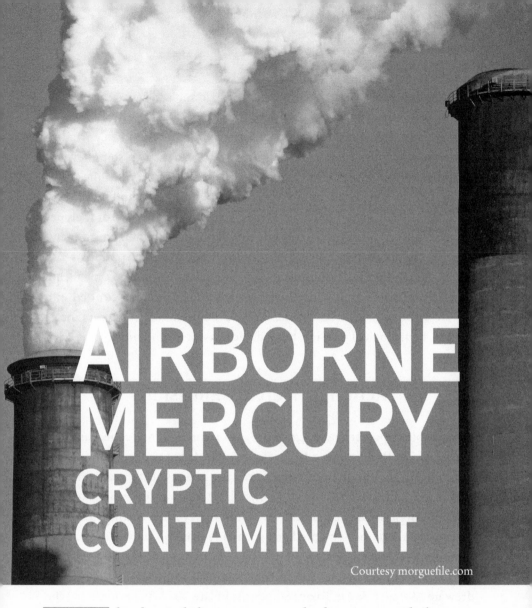

AIRBORNE MERCURY
CRYPTIC CONTAMINANT

Courtesy morguefile.com

The chemical element mercury, also known as quicksilver, was for centuries revered as the metal of the gods. The element was named for an ancient divinity, Mercury, a god who also had the good fortune of having a planet named after him by early astronomers. The Chinese regarded mercury as a miraculous substance, which could be used to restore health and prolong life. However, when an early Chinese emperor drank a concoction of powdered jade and mercury to secure eternal life, things did not work out so well. The emperor suffered liver failure and fatal mercury poisoning of his brain.[1]

We know today that mercury is highly toxic and can cause chronic and acute poisoning. That's why its use in thermometers, electrical switches, dental restorations, cosmetics, and fluorescent lights has been curtailed. Nevertheless, most Americans continue to be exposed to some level of the poisonous element. That's because airborne mercury continues to be released from mining operations, cement manufacturing, and the smoke-stacks of power plants. In fact, it's estimated that 65 percent of mercury emissions are from combustion facilities, with coal-fired electric genera-tion plants constituting the largest source of the hazardous pollutant.[2]

The major portion of electricity generated in Missouri comes from coal-fired plants, naturally raising concerns about mercury emitted into the air. Exposure to airborne mercury has been linked to cancers, heart disease, neurological damage, birth defects, asthma, and more.

Action on Mercury Emissions

Missouri's power plants emitted 3,835 pounds of toxic mercury into the air in 2010. According to Environment Missouri, just one gram of mercury falling into a twenty-five-acre lake is enough to make the fish unsafe to eat.[3] Health advisories against fish consumption from lakes and rivers in Missouri are common. Nevertheless, as of this writing, Missouri officials have not implemented any statewide controls on mercury as has been done in other states.

On a national level, the U.S. Environmental Protection Agency (EPA) drew up Mercury & Air Toxics Standards in late 2011. In announcing the standards, the EPA estimated the new safeguards would prevent as many as 11,000 premature deaths and 4,700 heart attacks annually. The stan-dards would also improve child health with 130,000 fewer cases of child-hood asthma symptoms each year. The EPA action on mercury and toxics was hailed as the most significant step to clean up pollution from power plant smokestacks since the 1990s Acid Rain Program.[4]

Support for EPA's Mercury Limits

Within months of the EPA's issuance of the mercury limits, Senator James Inhofe, R-Oklahoma, led a strident effort to invalidate the new standards. He was joined by forty-two other senators, who argued that the limits represented a war against the coal industry. Missouri senators split on the call for repeal of the EPA regulations. Republican Senator Roy Blunt sided with the Inhofe forces, while Democratic Senator Claire McCaskill allied with fifty-three senators who voted against relaxing standards on mercury and other airborne toxics.[5]

Many citizen, environmental, and religious groups joined in the fight to maintain the new EPA standards restricting mercury and toxic air pollution. More than 320 hunting and angling groups took a strong stand for cleaner air. An additional one thousand Missourians submitted comments to the EPA in support of the rule, along with more than a half million other Americans.[6]

Religious groups that expressed support of the new standards, and that opposed their repeal, included the U.S. Catholic Bishops Conference, the Jewish Council for Public Affairs, and the Evangelical Environmental Network (EEN). "The U.S. Senate did the right thing by rejecting efforts to kill mercury regulations at the expense of our children's health," said Reverend Mitch Hescox, president & CEO of EEN. "We've finally done the right thing by regulating mercury from power plants for the first time."[7]

Airborne Mercury Q & A

John Hickey is the Sierra Club's Missouri chapter executive director.

Q. Coal-fired power plants are a major source of mercury contaminants. How much do they emit and are there devices the plants can use to reduce mercury pollutants?

A. Coal-fired power plants are the single largest source of mercury pollution in the USA, emitting 130,000 pounds of toxic mercury pollution in 2009 alone. There is proven technology that can remove mercury from plant emissions; however, the utilities don't want to spend the money.

Q. Don't tall smokestacks on power plants like the Ameren electric plant in Labadie insure that mercury and other pollutants are dispersed until they are relatively harmless?

A. The tall smokestacks may transfer the poison to a more distant area, but it does not dilute the impact of the mercury, which accumulates as it moves up the food chain. The mercury that is polluting Missouri may come from coal-burning plants in Texas or Oklahoma.

Q. How does mercury get into fish in Missouri rivers and streams? Have Missouri agencies such as the Department of Natural Resources done enough to post warnings to anglers about the dangers?

A. Mercury is emitted by the coal-burning plant—the mercury comes out the smokestack and falls to the ground, where it bioaccumulates (i.e., smaller organisms absorb the mercury, and the mercury accumulates as it moves up the food chain, becoming concentrated in larger fish).

Q. Don't we have to accept some risk from mercury pollutants in exchange for readily available electricity?

A. Mercury pollution can be controlled with readily available technology. Note also that Ameren is currently selling 25 percent of its production "off-system" (i.e., outside its customer service area), due to Ameren's excess capacity. Finally, Ameren is currently not paying for health costs of mercury.

Q. Isn't there a risk assessment issue in play on mercury poisoning?

A. About one in six women of child-bearing age in the USA have too much mercury in their bloodstream to safely breastfeed their babies. That is unacceptable.

Notes

1. Wright, David Curtis, *The History of China* (Westport, Conn.: Greenwood, 2001), 48-50.
2. Wilson, Simon, "Global Anthropogenic Mercury Emission Inventory," *Atmospheric Environment* 40, no. 22 (July 2006): 4048-4063.
3. Mathys, Ted, "Mercury Standards to Face Attack in U.S. Senate Today," *Reporters Memo* (June 20, 2012).
4. Staff writers, "McCaskill, Blunt Divide on EPA Clean Air Rules," *Kansas City Star* (June 20, 2012): A1.
5. Mathys, 2.
6. Ibid.
7. Evangelical Environmental Network, "Evangelicals Praise Senate for Protecting the Unborn from Mercury Pollution," June 20, 2012, creationcare.org.

Additional Readings

Eisler, Ronald, *Mercury Hazards to Living Organisms* (New York: CRC Press, 2006).
Harris, Reed, *Ecosystem Responses to Mercury Contamination: Indicators of Change* (New York: CRC Press, 2007).
Pirrone, Nicola, *Mercury Fate and Transport in the Global Atmosphere: Emissions, Measurements and Models* (New York: Springer Publishing, 2010).
Zuber, Sharon L., and Michael C. Newman, *Mercury Pollution: A Transdisciplinary Treatment* (New York: CRC Press, 2011).

SULFUR DIOXIDE
MAKING TOP TEN LISTS

Photo by Max Bouvatte

T he American tribal love-rock musical, *Hair*, took up many contemporary themes of the 1960s when it debuted: the peace
movement, sexual liberation, environmental awareness and
the need to protect the natural world. A song from *Hair* struck
a chord with environmentalists with such sardonic lyrics as
"Welcome, sulfur dioxide / Hello, carbon monoxide / The air, the air / is
everywhere."

A character wearing a gas mask sang these words, and she lamented that dirty air was killing her with "vapor and fume at the stone of her tomb." The popular musical may now be a cultural artifact, but sulfur dioxide is still very much with us. The pollutant gas, the majority of which is produced by coal-fired plants, causes damage to both human health and the natural world.

Nature suffers especially when sulfur dioxide (SO_2) combines with precipitation to form acid rain. The resulting acidification of lakes, streams, and rivers can end their ability to support plant and animal life. Humans suffer a variety of respiratory illnesses from exposure to SO_2, including bronchitis and lung diseases. Congress reacted to these health concerns in 1990 when it passed amendments to the original Clean Air Act to curb emissions from power plants.[1]

Restrictions Difficult to Enforce

Missouri chapters of the Sierra Club and the Missouri Coalition for the Environment have been active on the issue of sulfur dioxide emissions in the state. At a Sunset Hills meeting of the Missouri Air Conservation Commission in 2012, SO_2 pollution got the top spot when Sierra Club members submitted their own pollution study along with requests for Department of Natural Resources (DNR) to operate sulfur dioxide monitors in Eastern Missouri.

"Ignorance is not bliss," said Sierra Club Missouri Chapter Executive Director John Hickey, regarding the lack of sulfur dioxide monitors. "We've got a public health crisis here. The science is clear. Sulfur dioxide limits are not being met. We can't keep putting our heads in the sand and say it isn't happening."[2]

The Sierra Club's report contends that the St. Louis region is exposed to dangerous levels of SO_2 from the stacks of two area plants operated by Ameren. Sierra Club members want regulators to install monitors in the vicinity of Missouri's largest sources of sulfur dioxide, Ameren Missouri's Labadie and Meramec plants. Members have produced an illustrated map and a report defining areas affected by sulfur dioxide plumes from coal-fired plants that produce electricity.

Utilities Respond to SO_2 Concerns

In response to Sierra Club concerns, an Ameren Missouri spokesperson said the utility has spent hundreds of millions of dollars on new technologies to remove sulfur dioxide and other pollutants from its plants for generating electricity.

"We believe the measures we've incorporated in our pollution control strategy will comply with all current and new EPA (Environmental Protection Agency) standards," said Michael Menne, vice president of Environmental Services Ameren Missouri. "These measures include installation of the SO_2 scrubber at our Sioux Energy Center, the use of ultra-low sulfur coal and enhanced particulate and mercury controls at our other energy centers in Missouri."[3]

Environmentalists are critical of smokestack scrubbers, which are designed to trap sulfur emissions before they reach the air so that they can be turned into sludge or solid waste. Scrubber technology is expensive, and critics argue that they only create a new problem of how to dispose of the waste byproducts. Efforts are being made to find ways to recycle the waste for commercial applications.[4]

Sulfur Dioxide Q & A

Sara Edgar is the Beyond Coal Campaign organizer for the Sierra Club.

Q. **What is sulfur dioxide? If it is produced naturally by volcanoes and forest fires, why do we have to worry about man-made sulfur dioxide?**

A. Sulfur dioxide (SO_2) is a strong-smelling colorless gas—or liquid when kept under pressure. Sulfur dioxide is produced by the burning of fuels that contain sulfur, such as coal and oil. Although it is naturally occurring, the largest producers of sulfur dioxide are man-made sources, which contribute to unhealthy levels of SO_2 in the air.

Q. **What is the impact of sulfur dioxide on humans?**

A. SO_2 is extremely harmful to health, especially when inhaled in the air. Exposure to SO_2 results in increased asthma symptoms, respiratory ailments, and decreased lung functioning.

Q. **St. Louis has been ranked in the Top 10 for sulfur dioxide pollution in recent years. Why is it in the Top 10?**

A. One of the reasons that St. Louis has such high levels of sulfur dioxide pollution is because of an over-reliance on coal for our energy production. St. Louis relies on coal for over 85 percent of our energy needs. Nationally, coal is used for less than 37 percent of the country's energy production.

Q. **Utilities have tried to limit sulfur dioxide pollutants from coal-fired plants with scrubbers. How effective is this technology?**

A. Scrubbers are said to be able to remove up to 90–95 percent of SO_2 produced by burning coal. However, since the SO_2 is no longer being emitted into the air, the scrubbers increase the amount of waste products left over from the burning of coal. Many of these waste products are considered harmful to health and lead to further complications with the disposal and reuse of these materials.

Q. Most of the sulfur dioxide is from electrical utilities. What other sources are there for this pollutant that affects St. Louis and Missouri?

A. Herculaneum lead smelter, trains, or other vehicles and equipment which burn high sulfur fuels.

Notes

1. Environmental Defense Fund: "A Timeline of the Clean Air Act," www.edf.org.
2. Corrigan, Don, "Residents Protest Smokestack Pollution," *South County Times* (July 6, 2012): 3.
3. Ibid.
4. Union of Concerned Scientists, "Environmental Impacts of Coal Power: Wastes Generated," www.ucsusa.org/clean_energy/coalvswind.

Additional Readings

Ackerman, Bruce, and William T. Hassler, *Clean Coal/Dirty Air: or How the Clean Air Act Became a Multibillion-Dollar Bail-Out for High-Sulfur Coal Producers* (New Haven: Yale University Press, 1981).

Freese, Barbara, *Coal: A Human History* (New York: Penguin Books, 2004).

Friedman, Thomas L., *Hot, Flat, and Crowded: Why We Need a Green Revolution—and How It Can Renew America* (New York: Picador, 2008).

MOSQUITO SPRAYING
SO LAST CENTURY

Courtesy morguefile.com

A dread Y2K virus, which would shut down vital computer systems and cause general global mayhem, never quite materialized as predicted at the turn of the millennium. However, a much-feared, mosquito-borne virus affecting humans did arrive on the East Coast in time for the Year 2000. The West Nile Virus's arrival was likened to the pestilence and plague that besieged Ancient Egypt. The ill effects of West Nile could include inflammation of the brain, accompanied by headaches, body aches, infection, convulsions, and even death.

The virus found its way to New York City in late 1999. By late 2001, medical experts said West Nile Virus had moved west and was impacting residents of Eastern Missouri. Dr. Mike Williams, manager for communicable disease control with St. Louis County Health Department, said the September 2001 arrival of West Nile Virus to the St. Louis area was a serious situation—a problem for St. Louis and Missouri—that was not going to go away.[1]

"There's a certain amount of panic out there, and that's unfortunate, because even though West Nile poses a serious situation, most people are not at great risk," said Williams. "We can react to reduce this problem. We can find new ways to attack the mosquitoes that spread West Nile Virus."[2]

Many area cities and the county reacted to the mosquitoes and the virus in "the old way" with fogging and spraying trucks. The method of attack was to use pesticides to kill the mosquitoes that carry the virus, thereby destroying the virus or, at least, limiting the threat. The 2002 spraying program kicked into high gear after county testing in Crestwood, Webster Groves, Sunset Hills, and Kirkwood all netted mosquito catches proving positive for West Nile.[3]

Problems with Pesticides

Many county residents were not pleased to see the trucks spraying in their neighborhoods. In 2003, the protesters came to city halls armed with a report on spraying from the Great Rivers Environmental Law Center. The center released a report contending that the county's program of "adulticiding" is the least effective means of mosquito control. The report also cited the county's use of Aqua-Reslin (an insecticide that uses the synthesized chemical neurotoxin known as permethrin) as a chemical containing agents known to irritate eyes, skin, nose, throat, and lungs.

Informed residents and environmentalists outlined three ways that the spraying was ineffective and harmful. First, the pesticides were known to have a direct effect on people's health by causing or agitating respiratory problems. Second, the mosquitoes that survive the spraying will adapt and breed generations that are more chemical resistant. Third, spraying kills off the mosquitoes' natural predators, whose populations find it much harder to recover from the eradication efforts. After all, mosquitoes have an average life span of one to two weeks and can breed and re-populate in a short amount of time.[4]

Environmentalists' objections harkened back to Rachel Carson's concern over the endocrine-disrupting chemical DDT. Carson, author of *Silent Spring* and founder of modern environmentalism, showed convincingly that DDT was destroying songbirds and other wildlife and creating a silent spring.

What Should Officials Do?

Kathleen Henry, president of Great Rivers Environmental Law Center, said the spraying is a problem because the chemicals in the sprays are lethal not only to mosquitoes, but also are highly toxic to cats, fish, frogs, birds, honeybees, and butterflies. She said use of insecticides has been linked with massive declines in honeybee populations across the country, and continued use of permethrin by the county will further endanger local honeybee populations.

The county should follow the Integrated Pest Management system advocated by the EPA and the Center for Disease Control (CDC), according to Henry. The program should focus on removal of breeding sites in public areas and educating residents on how to eliminate breeding sites in their yards. It should take into account natural ecosystem dynamics, including the effects of pesticides on non-target species and how natural predators can control mosquito populations.[5] The use of sprays is not sustainable, Henry said.

Mosquito Spraying Q & A

Kathleen Henry is president of Great Rivers Environmental Law Center

Q. How might the materials in mosquito spraying violate the Clean Air Act or the Clean Water Act?

A. The Environmental Protection Agency has acknowledged that permethrin spraying (a common chemical in mosquito spraying) results in contamination of streams and rivers, and this will force the Missouri Department of Natural Resources to require National Pollutant Discharge Elimination System permits under the Clean Water Act.

Q. Isn't there a risk assessment issue in play on mosquito spraying? Don't we have to accept some risk from the spray ingredients in exchange for getting rid of disease-carrying pests?

A. Concerns remaining to be addressed include: long-term human health risks of repeated spraying, impact on complex ecosystems, whether spraying may be counterproductive to eradicating WNV (West Nile Virus), the rate mosquitoes are developing resistance to sprays, and the efficacy of killing adult mosquitoes through indiscriminate spraying. Before responding to public alarm about WNV, government officials should carefully weigh the threats posed by WNV against the health costs of mosquito spraying.

Q. Austin, Texas, is famous for its bat population and for the doctor who brought in bats to eat malaria-carrying mosquitoes. Should St. Louis follow Austin's lead?

A. Bats are beneficial to the environment and do not cause the adverse effects to human health that mosquito sprays cause. St. Louis County should evaluate the studies on this issue and determine whether bats will help alleviate the problem in St. Louis.

Q. What are the costs of St. Louis County's mosquito spraying program?

A. For an ineffective treatment, in 2010 the county spent almost $96,000 on Aqua-Reslin, almost two-thirds of their overall insecticide budget. The total amount spent in 2010 counts only the permethrin itself, not the cost of purchasing, operating, and maintaining spray trucks, training and hiring employees to operate the spray trucks, or transporting, storing, and cleaning up the permethrin.

Q. **Is St. Louis County "acting like an autocrat," as some residents charge over the issue of mosquito spraying?**

A. Currently, one cannot opt out of spraying—the county has contracts with ninety-six of the ninety-eight incorporated municipalities within its boundaries, and it sprays permethrin in eighty-six of them. In addition, the only way a citizen can find out when his neighborhood will be sprayed is through an automated phone message that is updated every afternoon, meaning a citizen would need to call every afternoon to find out when his residence would be sprayed, and even then would only have several hours' notice.

Notes

1. Corrigan, Don, "The West Nile Virus: Like We Really Need Another Reason to Hate Mosquitoes," *Webster-Kirkwood Times* (May 3, 2001): 1.
2. Ibid.
3. Corrigan, Don, "Chemical Spraying: New Season, Renewed Concerns About Spraying for Mosquitoes," *South County Times* (June 13, 2003): 1.
4. Corrigan, Don, "Mosquito Spraying: St. Louis County Department of Vector Control Says Permethrin Kills Adult Mosquitoes and Leaves Little Residual Effect on Humans, Pets," *Webster-Kirkwood Times* (Sept. 6, 2002): 8.
5. Ibid.

Additional Readings

Patterson, Gordon, *The Mosquito Crusades: A History of the American Anti-Mosquito Movement from the Reed Commission to the First Earth Day* (New Jersey: Rutgers University Press, 2009).
U.S. Department of Health, "Toxicological Profile for Pyrethrins and Pyrethroids," www.atsdr.cdc.gov/ToxProfiles/tp155.pdf.
US EPA, "Permethrin Facts," www.epa.gov/oppsrrd1/REDs/factsheets/permethrin_fs.htm.
Virginia Technical University, "Study of Insecticide Neurotoxicity Yields Clues to Onset of Parkinson's Disease," www.cals.vt.edu/news/archives/20030324.php.
Webster, Barrie, "Sting Operation: No Spray of Hope," *The Globe and Mail* (May 1, 2003): 1.

SMOKING
THE ULTIMATE
INDOOR POLLUTION

B elching smokestacks are what many people think of when it comes to air pollution. Other images that may come to mind are thousands of tailpipes emitting carbon monoxide in a traffic jam. You may think of the thick contrails left by powerful engines of high-flying jets crisscrossing the skies. The American Lung Association, the Clean Air Council and other anti-pollution groups want you to give some thought to that single, solitary cigarette, weighing less than one gram, that may be wafting blue smoke your way.

A single cigarette smoked indoors is an incredible source of exposure to toxic pollutants. The pollutants come in concentrations indoors that exceed federal outdoor air quality standards devised for public health protection. Secondhand smoke reaches people from the end of a burning cigarette or from the person who breathes out inhaled smoke. According to the Clean Air Council, secondhand smoke contains more than four thousand chemicals, two hundred of which are classified as poisons and sixty-nine of which are known carcinogens.[1]

In 2010, the *Contra Costa Times* in California reported on the dangers of thirdhand smoke, which was described a year earlier in the journal *Pediatrics*.[2] Thirdhand smoke enters the body through skin exposure, dust inhalation and ingestion. A University of California at Berkeley study notes that thirdhand smoke pollution occurs when a thin layer of toxic substances from tobacco settle on surfaces long after the cigarettes have been consumed and extinguished.[3]

EPA Actions on Cigarette Pollution

The Environmental Protection Agency (EPA) has regulatory authority over outdoor pollution, but as of this writing has not filed any legal or regulatory actions for tobacco use violating its outdoor standards. In a 1992 report, *Respiratory Health Effects of Passive Smoke: Lung Cancer and Other Disorders*, the EPA did determine that tobacco smoke is a Group A Carcinogen that causes cancer in humans.[4]

Cigarette smoke presents more than just cancer risks. Additional health risks include cardiovascular and respiratory illnesses. These risks are a concern in the outdoor environment, but especially when concentrated indoors, not only for users, but for those passively absorbing both secondhand and thirdhand smoke.

Air quality studies nationally and in Missouri show that the presence of particulates and chemical carcinogens are both reasons to promote smoke-free environments. Secondhand smoke is pollution that causes about 3,000 lung cancer deaths and 37,000 heart disease deaths annually, according to the EPA. Smoke pollution is especially hard on young children. The EPA

estimates that secondhand smoke causes more than 150,000 hospitaliza-
tions for respiratory infections in children under eighteen months each
year in America.[5]

Missouri's Tobacco Report Card: "F"

Each year the American Lung Association issues a grade card on how
the nation and each state rates for tobacco control. For 2012, Missouri rated
an "F" in all four categories of Tobacco Prevention, Smokefree Air, Cigarette
Tax, and Cessation.[6] Missouri has always been in the lead among states with
the highest percentage of smokers. At the same time, Missouri has always
scraped the bottom with its low cigarette taxes.

In 2012, the American Cancer Society helped launch the Proposition
B 'Show-Me A Brighter Future Campaign' that would hike cigarette taxes
to raise funds for education and smoking cessation programs. Campaign
spokesperson Misty Snodgrass noted that smoking pollution cost the state
$2.1 billion annually in health care costs, $532 million of which is paid by
the state's Medicaid program.[7] When the votes were tallied on November
6, 2012, the antismoking proposal failed by a razor-thin margin, just as two
previous attempts at curbing smoking had failed since the year 2000.

Nicotine Q & A

Misty Snodgrass is a Legislative/Government Affairs Director for the American Cancer Society for Missouri.

Q. Why has it taken so long for cigarettes and tobacco smoke to be considered an environmental issue in the United States?

A. After the 1964 report from the Surgeon General linking lung cancer to smoking, the industry's response was to create doubt and they conducted a campaign of deception and disinformation for decades. The same strategy was repeated for secondhand smoke.

Q. Unlike environmental poisons such as dioxin or sulfur dioxide, tobacco's smoke is addictive. Does this make it an especially dangerous pollutant? How addictive is it?

A. Nicotine, the primary addictive agent in tobacco, can be introduced into the body through smoking or through smokeless tobacco products such as chewing tobacco, spit tobacco, snuffs, etc. where the nicotine is absorbed through the lining of the mouth.

  While nicotine is arguably more addictive than heroin, the amount of nicotine in secondhand smoke is considerably less than in the mainstream smoke directly inhaled by the smoker. The amount of nicotine in secondhand smoke would not be of as much concern as would the other two hundred-plus toxins.

Q. Industry lobbyists sometimes promote legislation that waters down regulations on emissions and protects polluters. What role do lobbyists play on the state level when it comes to tobacco?

A. At the national and the state level, lobbyists have been crucial to protecting tobacco industry interests at the expense of public health. A detailed study of lobbyist influence, "The Public Health Undermined," is available at http:/www.escholarship.org/uc/item/6m8626sk#page-1. According to reports filed at the Missouri Ethics Commission, the tobacco industry contributed over $250,000 to state elected officials in the 2010 campaign cycle.

Q. How have bans on smoking in workplaces benefitted employees? Are there immediate results that indicate health improvements in these work settings?

A. A 2008 study examined 371 bar workers from 72 bars one year after a smoke-free law was in effect for a year in Scotland. They found improvement in respiratory and sensory symptoms. Respiratory symptoms included wheezing, shortness of breath, morning cough, other cough, phlegm. Sensory symptoms included irritation of eyes, nose, and throat.

Q. Are there any new forms of cigarette substitutes that are less toxic for both the smoker and the environment?

A. There are a number of new tobacco products that have been introduced in the last few years. These include dissolvable tobacco products, such as Orbs (finely powdered tobacco pressed into a tablet and looks much like Tic Tac mints), gelatin strips (looks like breath freshening strips), and sticks that look like toothpicks. None of these have been tested for reduced harm. In the last couple of years electronic cigarettes, or e-cigarettes, have entered the market. The cardiovascular risks still remain and it should not be assumed they're less risky than cigarettes.

Notes

1. Clean Air Council, "Tobacco Smoke Pollution," www.cleanair.org/program/indoor_air/tobacco_smoke_pollution.
2. Bohan, Suzanne, "Thirdhand Smoke: Indoor Pollutants and Tobacco Resident," *Contra Costa Times* (February 18, 2010): 1.
3. "Thirdhand Smoke: Indoor Pollutant," articles.sun-sentinel.com/2010-02-18/health/sfl-thirdhand-smoke-021510_1_tobacco-smoke-carcinogens-indoor-air, 1-3.
4. Report Index, Major Conclusions, EPA: "Respiratory Health Effects of Passive Smoke: Lung Cancer and Other Disorders," www.epa.gov/smokefree/pubs/etsfs.html, 1.
5. Ibid.
6. American Lung Association, "National Smoking Report Card," www.stateoftobaccocontrol.org.
7. Corrigan, Don, "Supporters Say Tobacco Tax to Benefit Schools," *South County Times* (Oct. 26, 2012): 1, 3.

Additional Readings

Americans for Non-smokers' Rights, www.no-smoke.org.
Campaign for Tobacco Free Kids, www.tobaccofreekids.org.
Conway, Erik M., and Naomi Oreskes, *Merchants of Doubt: How a Handful of Scientists Obscured the Truth on Issues from Tobacco Smoke to Global Warming* (New York: Bloomsbury Press, 2011).
Proctor, Robert N., *Golden Holocaust: Origins of the Cigarette Catastrophe and the Case for Abolition* (Berkeley: University of California Press, 2012).
Tobacco Control Legal Consortium, www.publichealthlawcenter.org/programs/tobacco-control-legal-consortium.

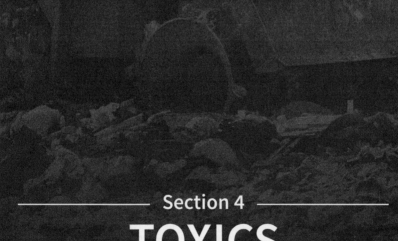

Section 4
TOXICS
WE CAN LIVE WITHOUT

Photo by Courtney Martin

"The shortsightedness of these environmental groups, in being concerned with 'controlling' rather than 'preventing' pollution, has encouraged the earth's continued destruction. These groups have failed to understand how various issues, such as ozone depletion, acid rain, toxic wastes, and harmful pesticides are interconnected but . . . continue to respond in a crisis mentality, bouncing from one trendy issue to the next."
—Penny Newman
"Killing Legally with Toxic Waste: Women and the Environment in the USA," 1994

t is easy to sympathize with environmentalists like Penny Newman, who are tired of compromise, tired of our calcified political process, tired of our seeming inability to address the big environmental problems we face. Some frustrated folks out there have turned to "everyday environmentalism," which involves grassroots efforts at "living green." Sustainable, green lifestyles are part of the solution to saving the planet, but major political and governmental actions are also required—legislative initiatives such as the Clean Air Act, the Strip Mining Act, and the Wilderness Act.

Composting yard waste and giving up bottled water are little steps in the right direction. However, these gestures do not address leaching poisons from tons of lead tailings; or the mounds of radioactive waste yet to find safe containment; or the growing pools of coal ash in danger of spilling into places where people are trying to simply live. These kinds of intractable problems involving toxics require a massive response—and will inevitably trigger push-back from powerful forces.

As a college newspaper adviser at Webster University in St. Louis for three decades, I sometimes watched my students challenge powerful entities with their stories about dioxin at Times Beach or radioactive waste at Weldon Spring. Their articles prompted an angry call to the university vice president about "these misinformed college newspaper articles" from a corporate director and university trustee. The vice president wisely suggested that the trustee member meet with the young reporters to explain the error of their ways.

At first, the university trustee chided and berated the student journalists, but they stood their ground—and stood by their stories. Near the end of the meeting, the trustee was apologizing for faulty judgments by his generation on the environmental front. He attributed mistakes to lack of good information and the exigencies of the Cold War. A rational discussion ensued. A dialogue began and finger-pointing—from both sides—diminished. Can we dream of a time when we all can engage in a dialogue about our big problems, such as toxics that threaten the planet, in the pursuit of rational solutions? At this point, we are still mostly dreaming.

Photo by Max Bouvatte

A NUCLEAR BURIAL GROUND

T he highest point in St. Charles County is not a bucolic, vine-covered bluff overlooking the Missouri River, but rather an enormous rock-covered mound that has been described as resembling an "ancient burial tomb."[1] Known officially as the Weldon Spring Site Remedial Action Project (WSSRAP), the forty-five-acre site is a tomb of sorts—for burial of some of the worst radioactive waste from the nuclear age. The tomb, completed in 2001, stores 1.5 million cubic yards of hazardous material.

Most Missourians are blissfully unaware that this tomb exists on the western edge of the St. Louis region, nor are they aware of their state's nuclear history that culminated in the tomb's creation. That history has been of keen interest to the Society of Environmental Journalists (SEJ), which selected the location near Weldon Spring, Missouri, for a study seminar when SEJ came to St. Louis in 1996.

Members of SEJ learned that the former Weldon Spring Ordnance Works manufactured seven hundred million pounds of TNT before the land became the site of a uranium ore processing plant in 1955. The plant processed raw uranium into "yellow cake" for nuclear warheads under the auspices of the Atomic Energy Commission (AEC). In 1966, the plant was suddenly closed and rumors of extensive radioactive contamination emerged. The U.S. Department of Energy (DOE) confirmed the rumors, as it found waste throughout the site with an estimated 214 tons of uranium and 129 tons of thorium.[2]

At the SEJ seminar session titled "After the Bomb, the Role of St. Louis," the audience learned that Mallinckrodt was the company authorized by the AEC to process the uranium, first at its north St. Louis plant, and then at Weldon Spring. When the Weldon Spring plant closed, the DOE eventually had to come up with a plan to contain the waste. The plan, which resulted in the giant "tomb," eventually came in with a price tag of $1 billion.[3]

A Billion-Dollar Debate

Environmental journalists assembled at Weldon Spring listened to a debate between anti-nuclear activist Kay Drey and Stephen McCracken, project manager for WSSRAP. McCracken defended the cleanup plan and entombing the radioactive waste on-site. Drey contended that the materials should be shipped to an isolated site away from populated areas. She also disputed the safety of the cleanup and the release of millions of gallons of contaminated water from the plant into the Missouri River. McCracken argued that the release of treated, diluted water was safer than leaving it in quarry ponds at the site.[4]

The WSSRAP cleanup plan was approved and the tomb now is in

place. Within the burial mound are barrels of uranium dust, pipes, clothing, trucks, and bulldozers in good working order that had to be abandoned. Atop the burial mound today is a viewing platform for visitors to the site. These visitors may want to start at the interpretive center before their climb, a building at the base where workers were once checked for radioactivity.[5]

Burial Tomb: End of Story?

Some might presume the burial tomb's completion means: end of story. Except the waste inside will remain radioactive for thousands of years beyond the effective life of the mound containment. What is more, not all the radioactive waste from the Mallinckrodt uranium processing operation made it into the tomb near Weldon Spring. Radioactive materials from Mallinckrodt's North Plant in St. Louis were scattered and dumped at sites throughout northwest St. Louis County.

Locations of radioactive waste include the St. Louis Airport Site, Latty Avenue Waste Site, and sites along Coldwater Creek and the West Lake Landfill Site. Longtime residents in the area of the Coldwater Creek sites report an unusual number of cancers, tumors, stillbirths, autoimmune disorders, and more health problems that they attribute to the presence of nuclear waste near their neighborhoods. "It's very disturbing trying to put the pieces together of why our friends are dying of horrid cancers," Jenell Rodden Wright told the *St. Louis Post-Dispatch* in 2013. She was interviewed for an article on lawsuits linking illnesses to wastes buried in Coldwater Creek neighborhoods.[6]

Radioactive Waste Q & A

Ed Smith agreed to answer these questions regarding radioactive waste in St. Louis. Smith is the safe energy director at the Missouri Coalition for the Environment.

Q. When the Weldon Spring contamination was being debated, some suggested the contaminated material be shipped off to isolated sites in Utah, rather than buried in our populated region. Does that make sense?

A. Storing radioactive waste on-site and transporting waste both present problems. It is likely that even if "all" of the wastes are assumed to have been removed, there would likely have been some that stayed. This would need to be monitored, possibly in the same way that is currently being done to ensure that the radioactive materials are not migrating into the surrounding environment. Transportation poses its own risks to the transportation crew and environmental damage in the case of a rail, truck, plane, or shipping accident.

Q. Do you see yourself as an activist on the radioactive waste issue, and other environmental issues for the foreseeable future? What have you learned from this experience?

A. One cannot put the blinders back on after learning about and working on these issues. Seeing the impact the radioactive contamination has had on people who live in affected communities is heartbreaking and the need for help in these communities is tremendous. I will continue my work, whether with the Missouri Coalition for the Environment or on my own, to help ensure that these radioactive wastes, especially at the West Lake Landfill, are remediated and will have as little impact on public health as possible.

Q. Was it a mistake to not transport radioactive wastes from places like the Latty Waste Site, Airport Site, and Coldwater Creek to Weldon Spring for burial in the mound project there?

A. No. It was a mistake to leave radioactive wastes at Weldon Spring, especially considering the significant population growth in that part of St. Charles County. Francis Howell High School is literally just hundreds of feet from the Weldon Spring site. Nuclear weapons' radioactive wastes belong at sites actually sanctioned to isolate these wastes from our environment.

Q. What is the safe solution for all these waste sites that dot northwest St. Louis County? Removal to other locations? Stabilization and monitoring of current sites?

A. The St. Louis Army Corps of Engineers has and will work to remove radioactive waste at sites in St. Louis City and County. So far the Corps has removed more than one million cubic yards of contaminated material to a federally sanctioned or licensed facility. The proper solution to radioactively impacted sites around St. Louis and beyond is to isolate and remove toxic materials from the environment, especially where there are lots of people.

Notes

1. Kaushik, T., "A Pile of Nuclear Waste Now a Tourist Attraction in Weldon Springs, Missouri," *Amusing Planet* (May 28, 2013): 1-7.
2. Corrigan, Don, "St. Louis Provides Field Day of Hazards," *St. Louis Journalism Review* (September 1996), 1.
3. Ibid.
4. Ibid.
5. Kaushik, 1-7.
6. Bernhard, Blythe, "Lawsuit links illnesses to St. Louis County creek," www.stltoday.com (Feb. 29, 2012), 1-4; www.stltoday.com/lifestyles/health-med-fit/fitness/lawsuit-links-illnesses-to-north-st-louis-county-creek/article_4d9b45ff-3aa2-560d-9ec9-8fa44436acfc.html.

Additional Readings

Bernstein, Jeremy, *Plutonium: A History of the World's Most Dangerous Element* (Sydney, Australia: University of New South Wales Press, 2009).

Kelly, D. D., *Radioactive Waste: Hidden Dangers* (New York: Rosen Publishing, 2006).

Murray, Raymond LeRoy, *Understanding Radioactive Waste* (Columbus, Ohio: Battelle Press, 1994).

Power, Max Singleton, *America's Nuclear Wastelands: Politics, Accountability, and Cleanup* (Pullman: Washington State University Press, 2008).

Zoellner, Tom, *Uranium: War, Energy, and the Rock That Shaped the World* (New York: Penguin, 2009).

DIOXIN SITES
IGNORANCE IS BLISS

T ake a trip to Route 66 State Park off of Interstate 44 in eastern Missouri and you may be tempted to hike or bike one of its seven miles of trails among the flora and fauna. However, such a temptation may dissolve after you learn a bit of environmental history about the 419-acre park, for here was once a town of two thousand residents known as Times Beach. In 1983, the Environmental Protection Agency (EPA) announced a buyout of the town and the evacuation of its residents. The federal buyout came after the discovery of incredible levels of the carcinogen dioxin in the soil of Times Beach.[1]

The shutdown of an American town for environmental reasons made headlines around the world, but so did the unlikely story of how the dioxin actually made it to Times Beach. A budget-strapped hamlet with dirt roads in the 1970s, the town contracted with waste hauler Russell Bliss to spray waste oil on the thoroughfares to keep the dust down. Bliss had a mix of oil and waste that came from a chemical plant in Verona, Missouri, that produced the defoliant Agent Orange for the Vietnam War. The waste clay and water from the Verona plant actually contained levels of dioxin some two thousand times higher than the content in Agent Orange, which was found to cause all kinds of illnesses among Vietnam War veterans returning home to the United States.[2]

Illnesses spawned by Bliss's toxic mix led to an EPA investigation and the town buyout. Times Beach was a ghost town for years, until the 1990s when a company called Syntex was contracted to burn the contaminated soil. High temperatures destroy dioxin and Syntex burned more than 250,000 tons of suspect soil at a cost of $110 million.[3] Some area residents wanted the burning stopped, fearing dioxin was coming out of smokestacks. Syntex dismantled its Times Beach incinerator after the dioxin assignment and the property was turned over to the State of Missouri, which converted it into a park.

Dioxin Capital of the World

In a 1994 article about Times Beach, *Riverfront Times* reporter C. D. Stelzer opened an exhaustive story with this lead: "It's been called the Watergate of molecules. Its poison trail winds through time, from the jungles of Vietnam to the Ozark hills. With more than two dozen confirmed dioxin-contaminated cleanup sites in Eastern Missouri, and a proposed dioxin incinerator at Times Beach, St. Louis could very well be considered the dioxin capital of the world."[4]

Times Beach was not the only Missouri site where Russell Bliss sprayed his dangerous oil and dioxin concoction. More than two dozen sites were identified. As the EPA made arrangements for these sites to be excavated and the ground transported to the Times Beach incinerator, more and more municipal officials became angered that this poisonous material would be transported through their towns. City officials downwind of the incinerator expressed concerns about what their citizens would be breathing.[5]

Almost two decades after the fires went out in the Syntex dioxin incinerator, many Missourians were breathing no easier about the "Watergate of molecules" inflicted on their state. Steve Taylor, who was active in the Times Beach Action Group (TBAG) of the 1980s, said he remains angry about the safety of the cleanup and the fact that no one was punished for making St. Louis "the dioxin capital of the world." He said Russell Bliss was not some innocent when he "killed horses, sickened children and threatened the health and well-being of residents with his despicable, illicit dumping activity."[6]

More Waste Barrels of Dioxin

Tammy Shea of Wildwood, Missouri, also remains skeptical about how dioxin—and those culpable for its spread—have been treated by local, state, and national officials. Shea has remained active and concerned about the dioxin issue ever since her time with the Times Beach Action Group in the 1980s. In 2012, she identified a number of barrels that she said had been left behind by the EPA at what is now known as the "Ellisville Site." They were among twelve-hundred barrels deposited on land once used by a truck driver employed by Bliss.[7] Shea is convinced that the massive cleanup job in the dioxin capital of the world is far from finished

Dioxin Q & A

Tammy Shea, a resident of Wildwood, Missouri, answered questions about dioxin and Times Beach.

Q. What was the name of the activist group that you became involved with over Times Beach and what was its mission?

A. I was involved with the Times Beach Action Group (TBAG), the organized effort of local citizens that opposed the construction and operation of the hazardous waste incinerator. The incinerator was recommended by the EPA as the remedial technology for the cleanup of twenty-seven Missouri sites. It was our goal to persuade the agency to consider alternative technologies that were demonstrated to be cleaner, safer, and less expensive than incineration.

Q. The EPA and state authorities debated whether to isolate dioxin in a bunker or burn it at Times Beach, so why did they choose incineration?

A. TBAG believed that the selection of incineration was driven by outdated information regarding safety. The resistance to alternatives was likely motivated by the fact that allowing independent analysis of the waste, a necessary step in selecting a remedial technology, would have revealed the presence of contaminants not factored into their risk assessment or their initial investigation.

Q. The Centers for Disease Control is revisiting what constitutes dangerous contamination levels—what does this mean in terms of Times Beach and St. Louis?

A. The EPA has been reviewing the toxicity of dioxin for more than a decade and just recently released new safety standards for noncancerous effects. The scientific advisory boards of the EPA and independent scientists have long advocated for a "no safe level" standard but that has not been instituted by the agency to date.

Q. Do you see yourself as an activist on the dioxin issue and other environmental issues for the foreseeable future? What have you learned from this experience?

A. Honestly, this issue has been on my watch list since about 1978. I first became curious about the family of dioxins when I began to hear reports about Vietnam veterans and their health problems related to Agent Orange exposure. I read reports published by Greenpeace around that time that described the political and corporate history of the chemical. This issue has dominated my entire adult life. I have often felt that this issue picked me, not the other way around. I will always be an advocate for a clean environment, but more important, an advocate for knowledge, freedom of information, truth, and accountability.

Notes

1. Corrigan, Don, *Show Me . . . Natural Wonders* (St. Louis: Reedy Press, 2007), 193.
2. Weiser, Kathy, *Ill-fated Times Beach* (Warsaw, Mo.: Legends of America, 2009), 1–2. See also: www.legendsofamerica.com/mo-timesbeach.html.
3. Ibid.
4. Stelzer, C. D., "Why Dioxin Is More Dangerous Than You've Been Told," *Riverfront Times* (May 18, 1994): 16.
5. Corrigan, Don, "A Dark Cloud Grows Over Times Beach;" *Webster-Kirkwood Times* (Oct. 21, 1988): 1, 5, 17, 18.
6. Taylor, Steve, "Bliss' Waste Dumping Killed Animals, Sickened Children," *St. Louis Post-Dispatch* (Sept. 19, 2012): B2.
7. Dere, Stephen, "Leftover Waste Barrels Spark Wildwood Debate," *St. Louis Post-Dispatch* (Dec. 28, 2012): A1, A8.

Additional Readings

Allen, Robert, *The Dioxin War: Truth and Lies About a Perfect Poison* (London: Pluto Press, 2004).
Gibbs, Lois Marie, *Dying from Dioxin: A Citizen's Guide to Reclaiming Our Health and Rebuilding Democracy* (Cambridge, Mass.: South End Press, 1999).
Schecter, Arnold, *Dioxins and Health Including Other Persistent Organic Pollutants and Endocrine Disruptors* (New York: Wiley, 2012).
Wilcox, Fred A., *Waiting for an Army to Die: The Tragedy of Agent Orange* (New York: Seven Stories Press, 2011).

COAL ASH
A FOSSIL FUEL FLAP

Photo by Max Bouvatte

C oal ash is an unavoidable by-product of coal-fired electric plants and always presents a storage or disposal problem. In Missouri, coal ash storage presents a big problem because the state has been up to 80 percent reliant on coal-fired plants for electricity. That problem has been magnified by a series of coal ash disasters around the country. There have been more than two hundred cases of coal ash spills in thirty-seven different states.[1]

Groundwater contamination by coal ash and disastrous spills were on the minds of environmentalists and concerned residents when they approached the St. Louis County Council in 2013. At issue: a potential coal ash landfill for Ameren's Meramec Energy Center coal-fired plant in Oakville near the juncture of the Meramec and Mississippi rivers. Residents asked county officials to take a stand against the proposed landfill and to demand that the Missouri Department of Natural Resources (DNR) start monitoring coal ash ponds now at the site for possible leakage and groundwater contamination.[2]

Air pollution from coal-fired plants usually produces tons of sulfur dioxide, which can cause heart problems, asthma attacks, and lung disease. However, contamination from coal burning does not only involve sulfur dioxide, but also chromium, arsenic, lead, and mercury. All these contaminants are listed as highly toxic, cancer-causing agents by the EPA.

Missouri environmentalist Sara Edgar, who attended the 2013 County Council meeting, said St. Louis County residents had reason to be concerned: "All of the news and controversy about coal ash landfills have been focused on the Ameren plant in Labadie on the Missouri River. But there should be some concern about a coal ash landfill plan in the Meramec River area. The potential for groundwater contamination or a serious spill is real."[3]

Labadie Plant in Franklin County

The coal-fired Labadie electric plant near Washington, Missouri, released the equivalent of 18.2 million metric tons of greenhouse gases in 2011, making it the fourth-largest emitter of greenhouse gases among U.S. industrial facilities. The plant data comes from an EPA database of greenhouse gas emissions from more than eight thousand industrial facilities.[4] However, area residents are not just concerned about what goes into the air, but also what may be going into the ground and the groundwater. They have been trying to stop a coal ash landfill proposed for Labadie on the nearby Missouri River.

"Our community has spent years fighting for protections for our drinking water, the floodplain and farmland from the leaking coal ash ponds and Ameren's proposal to permanently dump coal waste next to the ponds," said Patricia Schuba, president of Labadie Environmental Organization (LEO). "The decisions made on the Labadie coal ash landfill proposal could set a precedent for other communities contaminated by coal ash across the state of Missouri."[5]

Schuba made her comments at a joint press conference with the Sierra Club and the Missouri Coalition for the Environment in 2013. The Sierra Club's Sara Edgar told an audience in St. Louis that upward of 60 percent of drinking water in Missouri comes from the Missouri River. She stressed that when toxic wastes, from coal plants or otherwise, are dumped into floodplains, health is put at risk.[6]

TVA Coal Ash Spill

Edgar of the Sierra Club notes that anyone who wants to see what a coal ash landfill spill can look like should Google "TVA Coal Ash Spill." Internet images of the spill show rivers and property inundated by millions of cubic yards of gray, toxic, coal ash sludge.

The spill resulted after a landfill dike failed at the Kingston Plant near Knoxville, Tennessee, in 2008. TVA had dredged more than 3.5 million cubic yards of coal ash from local rivers as part of the cleanup by late 2012, but millions more cubic yards of toxic sludge remained.[7]

Coal Ash Q & A

Patricia Schuba represents the Labadie Environmental Organization (LEO). She agreed to answer the following questions.

Q. What is coal ash and how many of these utility waste sites do we have all over the country?

A. Coal ash is the waste left after the burning of coal; it contains approximately forty-four disease-causing chemicals that readily leach into water, such as arsenic, mercury, lead, chromium-6, and boron. As of June 27, 2012, we know of 1,161 coal combustion waste sites nationwide. There are at least 451 more coal ash ponds than previously acknowledged—significantly increasing the known threat from coal ash. The new data from the EPA indicates that at least 46 percent of CCW (coal combustion waste) waste ponds (535 ponds) operate without a liner, which would reduce the risk of leaching.

Q. Are Labadie folks concerned about a spill like the 1.1 billion gallon spill at the Kingston Plant in Tennessee, or is the major concern leaching?

A. The Labadie community is concerned both by the risk of site failure and water contamination. Like most CCW dump sites around the nation, the Labadie CCW ponds are located in a floodplain near a large river. The floodplain sediments are prone to liquefaction during an earthquake, to failure during flooding and earthquake shaking, and to water contamination both via groundwater and surface water. These risks predominantly endanger local drinking water but can also compromise the quality of Missouri River water that is used by the entire metropolitan St. Louis region.

Q. Floodplains have often been a dumping ground for unwanted materials. What are the problems with putting coal ash in a floodplain?

A. LEO argues that there are five major reasons to not dedicate limited floodplain land for CCW disposal: 1) health: increased risks of cancer, heart disease, autoimmune diseases, and neurological damage when groundwater becomes contaminated; risks are primarily due to leaching into water; 2) lost floodplain: reduced ability of the floodplain to filter water, hold floodwater, and grow safe food; 3) lost wetlands: lost habitat for other species; 4) unnecessary land use: floodplains should not be used for waste disposal and waste disposal in a floodplain is not necessary to the operation of an energy generation plant; 5) economics: a depressed economic zone about ten miles around high-risk sites, reducing property values, reducing opportunities for positive development.

It is our belief that the risks inherent in CCWs suggest that placement in floodplains or near water should be prohibited both by zoning law and in the yet to be released FEPA Coal Ash Rule.

Q. **What kinds of sustainable things might be done with this material—can it be mixed as an ingredient for concrete as some have suggested?**

A. Beneficially recycled CCWs are currently excluded from federal regulation under the EPA's May 2000 regulatory determination that the Bevill Amendment applies to such uses. When properly recycled and encapsulated, coal ash can be used in making such products as wallboard, concrete, roofing materials, and bricks. Currently we recycle about 50 percent of this waste, which reduces greenhouse gas emissions, conserves energy, reduces land disposal, and reduces the need to mine and process raw materials. Fly ash can be substituted for portland cement in the manufacture of concrete.

Notes

1. "We Need to Act," *St. Louis Post-Dispatch* (June 28, 2013): A14.
2. Corrigan, Don, "Reason to Blow Their Stacks," *South County Times* (July 12, 2013): 2.
3. Ibid.
4. Tomich, Jeffrey, "Labadie plant among top emitters of greenhouse gases," www.stltoday.com (Feb. 5, 2013), www.stltoday.com/business/local/labadie-plant-among-top-emitters-of-greenhouse-gases/article_951c0cff-c77d-5c5b-91b2-0d331bd4fb6f.html.
5. Rosenwasser, Emily, "Missouri Organizations Urge Protection of Missouri Floodplains from Dangerous Landfills," Sierra Club Press Statement, June 25, 2013.
6. Ibid.
7. Allyn, Bobby, "TVA held responsible for massive coal ash spill," *USA Today* (August 23, 2012), usatoday30.usatoday.com/news/nation/story/2012-08-23/tva-coal-ash-spill/57246824/1.

Additional Readings

Burns, Shirley Stewart, *Bringing Down the Mountains: The Impact of Mountaintop Removal on Southern West Virginia Communities* (Morgantown: West Virginia University Press, 2007).
Freese, Barbara, *Coal: A Human History* (New York: Penguin Books, 2004).
Goodell, Jeff, *Big Coal: The Dirty Secret Behind America's Energy Future* (New York: Mariner Books, 2007).
Shnayerson, Michael, *Coal River* (New York: Farrar, Straus and Giroux, 2008).

GETTING THE LEAD (POISONING) OUT

D angerous dust and grime from old lead paint are not fit for ingestion by man or beast, because this detritus is highly toxic. Concern over the presence of such toxins was obvious in 2009 when horses and police officers were removed from the mounted patrol division stables at Forest Park in St. Louis. Tests found high levels of lead on the stable's floor and loft.[1] The structure, built in 1919, was closed for remediation after crews, who were at work to repair the roof, discovered elevated levels of lead from the weathered lead paint that had been used on the roof.

Unfortunately, the contamination found at the stables is only a small part of the lead story in St. Louis. The Gateway City gets prominent mention in any study of lead poisoning in the United States. That is because St. Louis ranks high in such poisoning vis-à-vis other cities in the United States. For example, county-level data from 2009 shows the prevalence of childhood lead poisoning in Cuyahoga County (Cleveland) at 2.83 percent; Hamilton County (Cincinnati) at 1.01 percent; Marion County (Indianapolis) at 0.61 percent; and St. Louis City (which is not part of a county) at 3.24 percent.[2]

In urban areas, it is not an issue of lead mining, lead smelters, or lead tailings—it is all about the housing stock. In St. Louis, many of the homes are older, with lead paint and its dust affecting the occupants, particularly children. Homes built before 1978 likely have at least some lead-based paint in room ceilings and window frames. Lead dust from the painted surfaces is absorbed from the air by breathing it. In some cases, children have been known to eat paint chips and the poisoning can be a chronic problem.

Painting a Grim Picture

For the first half of the twentieth century, paints contained high amounts of lead to make them more durable so they would adhere to areas of high traffic and exposure to moisture. However, concern over health effects of lead prompted federal regulation of the material in paint by 1972, and by 1978 it was effectively banned in residential paints.[3] Also in the late 1970s, lead was removed from gasoline under the U.S. Clean Air Act.[4]

Ill effects from absorbing lead are many, and babies and children especially suffer after ingesting lead. In her book, *Children and Pollution: Why Scientists Disagree*, Colleen F. Moore contends that children with high levels of lead in their bodies suffer from brain malfunction, learning disabilities, inhibited growth, hearing issues, and chronic headaches. Of course, lead also harms adults by causing muscle and joint pain, hypertension, nervous system disorders, and more.

According to Moore, the net gain in health from reducing lead content in homes far outweighs the costs of any removal procedures. She cites a Centers for Disease Control (CDC) study that argues that reduction in lead exposure would save thousands of dollars per child in special education and medical costs. "These savings are just dollars—there would also be a lot of heartbreak saved for parents who avoid the agony of having a child who just cannot do well in school, has behavior problems, or has developed seizure disorder after lead poisoning."[5]

Abatement and Remediation

Matt Steiner, a health department epidemiologist with the City of St. Louis, notes that up until 2003, an alarming number of children younger than age six were poisoned by lead. However, the introduction of the Lead Safe St. Louis program gradually reduced the incidences of poisoning. The goals of Lead Safe St. Louis are to test every child for lead poisoning, to test homes for the prevalence of lead contamination, and to make assistance available for lead abatement or remediation.

Abatement involves getting rid of lead totally by removing home components, such as window frames, which are contaminated with lead. Steiner said abatement can be extremely costly and may be an unrealistic option. He said remediation, which can involve sanding away contaminated areas and tamping the area down with several coats of safe paint, can be effective and less costly.

Lead Q & A

Jeanine S. Arrighi, MS, MPPA, is a health services manager for children's environmental health with the City of St. Louis Department of Health. She has authored a number of reports on childhood health issues, and drew from some of these studies for her responses to these questions.

Q. What is lead poisoning and what are its impacts?

A. Exposure to lead in housing poses a significant health risk to young children. When absorbed into the body, it is highly toxic to many organs and systems and seriously hinders the body's neurological development. Lead is most harmful to children under age six because it is easily absorbed into their growing bodies and interferes with the developing brain and other organs and systems.

Q. How do lead contamination rates in St. Louis compare to those in other major urban areas?

A. In 2010, 29,476 children aged six and under—out of a total population of 319,294 according to the 2010 census—lived in the city, and 421 had blood lead levels with an SPR [screening prevalence rate] of 3.0 percent. The SPR rate both nationwide and in Missouri is about 1.2 percent

---

Q. Lead poisoning affects the young in particular in St. Louis. How does it get into their systems?

A. Most children with elevated lead levels are poisoned in their own homes by peeling lead-based paint and the lead dust it generates. Lead dust settles quickly, is difficult to clean up, and is invisible to the naked eye. Young children usually are poisoned through normal hand-to-mouth activity, as lead dust settles on their toys and the floor.

Q. What laws are on the books to address the lead contamination issue?

A. It is difficult for the federal government to enforce the laws it has in place. City agencies are involved with lead poisoning prevention work with federal agencies where feasible to inform them of needed enforcement. One ordinance the St. Louis Building Division is currently trying to expand is the Housing Conservation District program. The effort is intended to include the entire city in pre-occupancy inspections, through which the Building Division can identify and cite owners for peeling paint. If the paint is not repaired, the property may be referred for a full lead inspection.

Q. What problems confront the St. Louis testing and abatement programs when it comes to lead contamination?

A. The biggest impact to our programs is declining resources. Congress cut CDC's (Centers for Disease Control) lead program funding from $29 million to $2 million in 2012. We will no longer receive about $35,000 per year via the Missouri Department of Health and Senior Services's grant funding from the CDC. Less HUD (Housing and Urban Development) lead hazard control funding is available as well.

Notes

1. "Mounted Patrol Stables Renovation Underway," *West End Word* (July 5, 2013): 13.
2. www.cdc.gov/nceh/lead/data/state.htm.
3. Moore, Colleen, *Children and Pollution: Why Scientists Disagree* (New York: Oxford University Press, 2009), 3–35.
4. Ibid.
5. Ibid.

Additional Readings

English, Peter C., *Old Paint: A Medical History of Childhood Lead-Paint Poisoning in the United States to 1980* (New Jersey: Rutgers University Press, 2001).
Markowitz, Gerald and David Rosner, *Lead Wars: The Politics of Science and the Fate of America's Children* (Berkeley: California Milbank Books, 2013).
Warren, Christian, *Brush with Death: A Social History of Lead Poisoning* (Baltimore: The Johns Hopkins University Press, 2001).

METHANE
LIGHTING UP
LANDFILLS

Photo by Courtney Martin

The late Missouri environmentalist Roger W. Taylor lamented the number of landfills in the St. Louis area in his ode to a more pristine era titled *Born in the County*. His 1995 book pointed out how years of trucks dumping garbage in county landfills, as well as used oil, tires, batteries, appliances, and yard waste, had created intolerable situations for neighboring communities. Laws regulating the landfills were being violated and the stench was becoming a scandal.

Even worse than the odor was the presence of toxics such as benzene and mercury. Vast amounts of methane, carbon dioxide, and other greenhouse gases also were being emitted by these unsightly mountains of garbage. The mountains themselves were becoming some of the highest points in the county and violated the height limits set by the Department of Natural Resources (DNR). Taylor wrote about nearby tree die-offs and fears that vents installed to burn off excess gases on the mounting landfill dumps might not be enough to stave off methane explosions.[1]

Taylor balanced his 1995 criticism of eastern Missouri's hills of trash with some hope for the future. He noted that state and county governments eventually passed restrictions on what could be put in the landfills in order to make them safer. Taylor also lauded recycling efforts and municipal waste management programs to reduce the need for landfills. He cited expert views that the landfills would last no more than ten or fifteen years and then would be closed.[2]

Horizons Full of Landfills

More than fifteen years after Taylor's observations on the limited life span of landfills, reports of their likely demise now seem to be greatly exaggerated. Landfills in Earth City and east of Valley Park in Missouri are growing by the day. A giant landfill along Interstate 70 in Illinois, just northeast of the St. Louis Gateway Arch, dwarfs the nearby ancient Cahokia Mounds tourism and archaeological destination. A landfill north of this site, just east of the old Chain of Rocks Bridge, is spotted with eternal flames burning off methane.

A dump in Bridgeton, Missouri, began making television news and newspaper headlines in 2013 due to foul odors from smoldering trash. The stench caused headaches, nose and throat irritations, and breathing difficulties for nearby residents. The odor reached such extremes that Republic Services, owner of the fifty-two-acre landfill, offered free hotel stays to residents within a one-mile radius of the stinking mess.[3]

The Bridgeton Landfill took waste from 1985 to 2004, and sometime after that, the debris beneath the surface of the pile began to heat up and then ignited to create hideous odors. Missouri Attorney General Chris Koster demanded that the fire be extinguished and, under an agreement reached with Republic, the company was obligated to contain the fire; test all leachate runoff for toxins and dispose of them properly; pay for daily air-quality monitoring; and make plans for a permanent cap to be placed on the landfill.[4]

Radioactive Landfill Threat?

As the Bridgeton Landfill continued to smolder in the summer of 2013, the Missouri Coalition for the Environment (MCE) began to warn that the smelly fire threatened to become something much worse. MCE and other environmental organizations expressed concern that the landfill fire was located only twelve hundred feet away from radioactive waste left behind in the West Lake Landfill.[5]

Environmentalists also cited a report by California engineer Todd Thalhamer, a nationally recognized landfill fire expert, who found cause for alarm about radioactive waste being so close to the fire. According to Thalhamer's read on the situation, a barrier needed to be constructed between the fire and an area known as the north quarry containing the radioactive waste in West Lake.[6] As of this writing, there were no plans to act on Thalhamer's recommendation for a barrier between the landfill fire and the radioactive waste.

Landfills Q & A

Peter Anderson and **Kathleen Logan Smith** answered the following questions about landfills. Anderson is the executive director of the Center for a Competitive Waste Industry. Logan Smith is director of environmental policy with the Missouri Coalition for the Environment (MCE).

Q. Are most of the large visible landfills in the St. Louis area filled with garbage collected by waste trucks from people's homes?

A. Institutional waste is also a huge contributor, especially from hospitals, universities, factories with shipping operations, and more. Landfills often also take certain demolition and construction waste. It is a smorgasbord. Some take disinfected biomedical waste.

Q. In 1995, some experts estimated that all area landfills would be full and closed by 2005 or 2010. What happened? How much life does a landfill normally have?

A. Recycling programs did play a role in reducing the volume headed for landfills. The ban on organic materials in landfills, which meant keeping out leaves, sticks, logs, and grass, helped a lot with both volume and the problem of excessive methane generation.

Q. What are some of the more dangerous toxics posed by landfills? Is there oversight on what gets dumped?

A. Methane gas is obvious. In a landfill fire, dioxin also is an issue. Also, it matters what is dumped there. At West Lake in the Bridgeton area, they are finding all kinds of chemicals. No one really watches what gets dumped in a landfill. Really. There is no independent oversight to speak of.

Q. The underground fire at the Bridgeton Landfill has been in the news for months. How does this smoldering start? Why is it so hard to put out?

A. The landfill's owner, Republic, tried to save money and refused to install a proper cover on the landfill. It also refused to install liners and so it probably generates three times the methane of a traditional landfill. As that gas migrated laterally underground into adjacent basements, which created the risk of explosions, they were required to install gas collection piping to extract that gas. But, without a seal on top, they also pulled air, which appears to have ignited the methane. In general, landfill fires cannot be extinguished. They smolder with very little oxygen so the goal is to cut off all the oxygen. Adding water or air to them tends to make the problem worse.

Notes

1. Taylor, Roger W., *Born in the County: Stories and Songs* (Ballwin, Mo.: Kestrel Productions, 1995), 85–91.
2. Ibid.
3. Bernhard, Blythe, "Landfill Offers Area Residents Stay in a Hotel," *St. Louis Post-Dispatch* (May 8, 2013): A1, A5.
4. Bernhard, Blythe, "Landfill Owner Will Cap Site to Stop Smelly Fire," *St. Louis Post-Dispatch* (May 15, 2013): A1, A7.
5. Navarro, Heather, "MCE Speaks . . . DNR Responds," Missouri Coalition for the Environment Release, March 26, 2013.
6. Tomich, Jeffrey, "State Yet to Act on Advice to Contain Landfill," *St. Louis Post-Dispatch* (June 20, 2013): A1, A3.

Additional Readings

Rathje, William and Cullen Murphy, *Rubbish! The Archaeology of Garbage* (Tucson: University of Arizona Press, 2001).
Strasser, Susan, *Waste and Want: A Social History of Trash* (New York: Holt Paperbacks, 2000).
Tammemagi, Hans Y., *The Waste Crisis: Landfills, Incinerators, and the Search for a Sustainable Future* (New York: Oxford University Press, 1999).

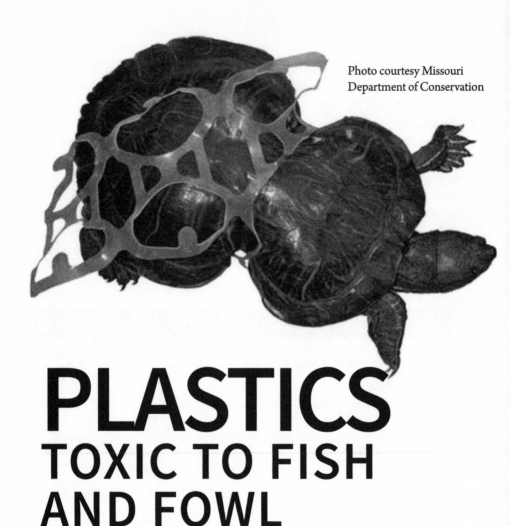

PLASTICS
TOXIC TO FISH
AND FOWL

t is called "green fishing," but it is not about reeling in some gleaming
fish with green gills, nor about angling on the famous Green River favored by Creedence Clearwater Revival. Green fishing is about environmentally sound approaches to enjoying the water and the outdoors.
When it comes to fishing, it means choosing eco-friendly tackle: biodegradable fishing line rather than plastic, corks rather than plastic bobs, sink-
ers that are not simply lugs of lead. It also means packing everything up and
out after a fishing trip—and not leaving plastic six-pack holders behind that
tangle and choke wildlife.

It is not necessary to go to the East or West coasts to see the damage done to marine life by plastic refuse. The Missouri Department of Conservation (MDC) actually has its own wildlife poster child who exhibits the deleterious effects of plastic pollution. The mascot for the "No More Trash" campaign in Missouri is none other than Peanut the Turtle, a red-eared slider turtle found with a plastic ring stuck around her body in 1993. This caused her shell to grow into the unusual figure eight for which she was named.

"Peanut was discovered in the Busch Conservation Area of St. Charles County and taken to the St. Louis Zoo where X-rays were taken. She had a collapsed lung besides the unusual shape," explained Dan Zarlenga of MDC. "We took her from the zoo and now she is the official mascot for the Missouri Department of Conservation and Transportation's 'No More Trash' campaign."[1]

Long Way to Go

Although Peanut has been enlisted in the fight against pollution for a score of years, Zarlenga noted that it is hard to know if the turtle has put much of a dent in the problem. Presently, each Missouri resident generates about 4.3 pounds of waste and trash each day. Millions of pounds of garbage find their way into the environment in the state on an annual basis. Trash comes in many forms and the varieties vary in how long they take to decompose. A paper bag can take a month; a disposable diaper can take 250 years; an aluminum can will take 500 years; and some plastics can take up to a million years.[2]

"The Missouri Department of Transportation spends $5.8 million annually just to clean litter from state highways," explained Zarlenga. "If people stopped throwing litter out their car windows, that money could be spent improving Missouri roads."[3]

Missouri highway patrol and state conservation agents write thousands of tickets a year for those who litter. But no amount of fines paid will bring back the wildlife that perishes because of the impact of litter on habitat.

Zarlenga emphasized that plastic needs to be recycled. Plastic that gets put in the trash ends up in landfills, where it lasts forever and where it can be washed out during storms into streams and rivers. There is tremendous runoff in urban areas now, because of all the impervious surfaces. Roofs, parking lots, highways, and sidewalks all create runoff that carries pollutants and trash into waterways where wildlife is already experiencing survival problems.

National and Global Issue

According to Lori Diefenbacher, coordinator of the Education for Global Sustainability program at Webster University in St. Louis, the effects of plastic litter on wildlife are especially insidious. She said scientists see it as an international issue with a need for global treaties to address the problem. She added that plastic pollution now has become problematic, not only for oceans, but in waterways generally.

"Most of us know how plastic chokes, strangles, and traps animals, but the toxicity of both the polymers and the chemical additives to the plastic cause health and pollution problems as well," she stressed. Diefenbacher said people need to cut down on buying items with plastic packaging. They should also recycle plastic items and be aware that, as litter, it is not just unsightly, it is illegal and can kill.[4]

Plastics Q & A

Lori Diefenbacher is coordinator of the Education for Global Sustainability program in the School of Education at Webster University. She agreed to answer these questions on plastic pollution and dependency on plastics.

Q. Where did our dependency on plastics start?

A. I grew up on plastic—my dad was a plastics engineer—and we argued endlessly about the problems. He and many others considered the product a solution to other disappearing resources—tortoiseshells, shellac, ivory, etc.—and I know firsthand that they did not anticipate the complications.

Q. Most plastics, such as bottles and containers, are still ending up in landfills. Is there a way to encourage more recycling?

A. I am a teacher of teachers, so of course the answer to this is "education." If we begin modeling and teaching recycling with preschoolers and maintain that philosophy throughout a child's student career, the practice of recycling would spread exponentially. I keep thinking that recycling is institutionalized, but then I go to an airport with no recycling containers or visit a school where there are only two bins in the building. We have a very long way to go with this paradigm shift. People want to do the right thing, but only if it is convenient.

Q. The Plastic Pollution Coalition (PPC) insists that recycling plastics is not doing the job for the environment, that we simply need to end plastic dependency. Do you agree?

A. I believe we have a responsibility to reduce our dependency on plastic and to aim for an end to that dependency, but the PPC uses the Internet to get its message out to people . . . how much plastic is in their computers? How many of them drive cars? It is easy to say we should end dependency, but plastic is so integrated into our material world, it would be difficult. There are many things that can be eliminated easily. We could do with a lot less food packaging; plastic single-use bags and bottles are an easy target.

Q. What are the effects of plastics on flora and fauna? We have all seen the photos of sea turtles tangled up in plastic—what happens in our own backyards?

A. Microplastics, which in part come from the repeated washing of synthetic fabrics, are present in oceans and most freshwater. Of course, this means that the plastic components are leaching into the food chain as well.

Notes

1. Corrigan, Don, "Turtle Is Mascot Against Litter," *Webster-Kirkwood Times* (March 1, 2013), B1, B10.
2. Ibid.
3. Ibid.
4. Ibid.

Additional Readings

Allison, Rachel Hope, *I'm Not a Plastic Bag* (Chicago: Archaia Entertainment, 2012).
Humes, Edward, *Garbology: Our Dirty Love Affair with Trash* (New York: Avery Penguin Books, 2012).
Knight, Geof, *Plastic Pollution* (Mankato, Minn.: Heinemann-Raintree, 2012).
Terry, Beth, *Plastic-Free: How I Kicked the Plastic Habit and How You Can Too* (New York: Skyhorse Publishing, 2013).

PCBs

DETECTING DAMAGING DATA

Veteran St. Louis Cardinals fans, who recall going to the old Sportsman's Park to watch Stan Musial whack out singles and doubles, may remember a bustling factory in the park's north-side neighborhood. The Carter Carburetor plant on North Grand Boulevard employed as many as three thousand people until it shuttered in 1984. From the 1930s to the mid-1980s, the brick and glass factory noisily manufactured carburetors. Then it closed.

After sitting empty for three decades, the once thriving industrial site has become more than just a crumbling eyesore. The dilapidated plant is an EPA site. The major environmental hazard that needs millions of dollars in removal costs: PCBs (polychlorinated biphenyls). Cancer-causing PCBs were left behind by hydraulic fluid used in die-cast machines, according to a May 2011 report in the *St. Louis Post-Dispatch*.[1]

The PCB-tainted factory in Missouri is not an isolated location for dangerous amounts of polychlorinated biphenyls. According to reasonable estimates, 1.5 million pounds of PCBs were produced from 1929 to 1989, a large portion of which ended up in the environment.[2] Many buildings in the United States with known PCB contamination have been evacuated, sealed, and locked down. A large amount of PCB waste from electrical transformers, capacitors, and other components has ended up in municipal landfills. These sites are not designed to keep PCBs from finding their way into the atmosphere or groundwater. Often these sites have been sealed and posted with warning signs.

What Are PCBs?

Polychlorinated biphenyls were once manufactured for use as highly stable coolants in devices that might heat to dangerous temperatures, such as transformers and electric motors. They also were used as lubricants in items such as paint, plastics, adhesives, fire-retardant fabrics, and inks. As employees involved with the manufacture of these items began to develop chloracne and symptoms associated with hepatitis, PCBs were tracked as the culprit. PCB production was banned by the U.S. Congress in 1979 and subsequently by the Stockholm Convention on Persistent Organic Pollutants in 1997.[3]

In her study of PCBs, award-winning French journalist Marie-Monique Robin interviewed Professor David Carpenter, director for the Institute of Health and the Environment at the University of Albany. Carpenter told Robin: "We all have PCBs in our bodies. They belong to a category of twelve very dangerous chemical pollutants known as persistent organic pollutants—POPs—because, unfortunately, they are resistant to natural biological decay and they accumulate in the living tissue throughout the entire food chain."[4]

According to Carpenter, regular exposure to PCBs can lead to liver, pancreatic, intestinal, breast, lung and brain cancer, cardiovascular disease, hypertension, diabetes, immune deficiency, thyroid disease, and serious neurological diseases. Add to this list certain reproductive problems, sexual hormone imbalance, and endocrine disruption.

Cleaning Up PCB Messes

Efforts have been made to remediate contaminated sites and to destroy concentrations of PCBs across the United States and around the world. The task is not an easy one, because PCBs do not oxidize and readily decompose in the natural environment. In the United States, attempts at remediation are still under way at sites along the Hudson River and the Great Lakes, as well as in Massachusetts, North Carolina, South Carolina, and Alabama.

The contamination in St. Louis has been cited as an especially difficult case for cleanup, because the PCBs have infiltrated the ground perhaps as deep as thirty feet. The Missouri Coalition for the Environment's Kathleen Logan Smith notes: "Everybody wants it cleaned up. But they have not done this anywhere with contamination at this level."[5]

PCBs Q & A

Pat Costner and **Steve Taylor** were both activists during the Times Beach contamination controversy. Costner serves as a senior science adviser to the International POPs (Persistent Organic Pollutants) Elimination Network. Taylor is a mathematician and communicator, who served as a congressional spokesperson for former U.S. Representative Todd Akin of Missouri.

Q. Polychlorinated biphenyls (PCBs) were banned by the United States in 1979 and by the Stockholm Convention in Europe in 2001. Has this made the environment safer and healthier?

A. It is important to distinguish between PCB production and PCB use. PCB production ceased globally more than a decade ago, but much PCB-containing equipment remains in use. Materials containing PCBs are often still awaiting proper disposal.

Q. What harmful health effects led to their being banned?

A. Acute PCB poisoning can lead to kidney failure, and PCBs have been strongly linked to some forms of cancer. They belong to a class of chemicals believed to adversely affect human immune and endocrine systems.

Q. Why were PCBs made in the first place and for what purposes were they manufactured?

A. PCBs have been used in sealants, caulks, paints, adhesives, as flame retardants in fabrics, and for electrical insulation. Industries wanted a heat transfer medium and lubricant that was effectively indestructible. PCBs were produced in the St. Louis area, and Monsanto Company was a major manufacturer of PCBs at one time.

Q. Old factories, abandoned industrial lands, and waste ponds are contaminated with PCBs, and many of these sites are in urban areas like St. Louis. Why are they so persistent and why have they not been cleaned up?

A. PCBs are, as intended, extremely persistent. They are resistant to chemical, physical, and biological processes that can be expected to break them down. The processes for determining the presence of PCBs are expensive, as are the methods for destroying PCBs in materials, sediments, and soils.

Q. PCBs are found in old electrical transformers and other equipment. Does this mean that antique radios in the basement can be a source of danger to a family?

A. Unfortunately, PCBs can be found in many things and are ubiquitous, so some exposure may be unavoidable. It is important to reduce exposure, especially given the bioaccumulative nature of these compounds. It would be best to consult the EPA for guidance in disposing of old electrical equipment.

Q. What is meant by the term midnight dumping and how does this account for PCB-laced materials ending up in waste dumps where they do not belong?

A. Midnight dumping has always been a way of illegally getting rid of unwanted waste materials, sometimes under the cover of night, or otherwise surreptitiously. However, PCB-contaminated materials are commonly unidentified or deliberately misidentified. They are sent, knowingly or unknowingly, to dumps, salvage yards, and landfills.

Notes

1. Tomich, Jeffrey, "Toxic Site Cleanup Is Short on Action," *St. Louis Post-Dispatch* (May 12, 2011): A1, A7.
2. Moore, Colleen F., *Children and Pollution: Why Scientists Disagree* (New York: Oxford University Press, 2009), 68–103.
3. Ibid.
4. Robin, Marie-Monique, *The World According to Monsanto* (New York: The New Press, 2010), 22–29.
5. Tomich, A1, A7.

Additional Readings

Dracos, Theodore Michael, *Biocidal: Confronting the Poisonous Legacy of PCBs* (Boston: Beacon Press, 2012).
Egginton, Joyce, *The Poisoning of Michigan* (East Lansing: Michigan State University Press, 2009).
Hansen, Larry G. and Larry W. Robertson, *PCBs: Human and Environmental Disposition and Toxicology* (Champaign: University of Illinois Press, 2008).

RADON GAS

DANGER
RADON GAS

INVISIBLE MENACE

Not all dangerous contaminants come out of a drain pipe, a spray nozzle, or a smokestack. Not all contaminants are man-made materials that are grossly mishandled. In the case of radon, we are talking about a toxic gas that occurs naturally and results from the breakdown of uranium and other radioactive materials in the soil and rocks. Because radon is impossible to see or smell, many people are exposed to it every day without ever knowing the effects it can have on them. Such exposure can cause DNA damage and lung cancer.

The EPA has estimated that as many as twenty thousand lung cancer fatalities are caused each year by radon. Radon is the second leading cause of lung cancer after cigarette smoking—and the combination of smoking and radon exposure is especially deadly. According to the EPA, a family whose home has radon levels of 4pCi/l (picocuries per liter) is exposed to about thirty-five times as much radiation as the Nuclear Regulatory Commission (NRC) would permit if a family was standing next to the fence of a radioactive waste site.[1]

Radon can be found all over the United States. In Missouri, the highest concentrations appear to be in the northwest part of the state and southeast portions of the state, excluding the bootheel area. The Kansas City and St. Louis areas both have zip codes where the risk of radon is elevated.[2] Although some level of radon is always present in the outdoors, the toxic gas becomes problematic when it accumulates in the interior of buildings— homes, offices, and schools. The gas typically seeps through foundation cracks, construction joints, gaps around pipes and utility points of entry, and faulty wall construction.

Cancer Survivors Against Radon

Gloria Linnertz, a member of Cancer Survivors Against Radon (CanSAR), has worked with state legislators in both Missouri and Illinois to pass laws related to real estate agent disclosure of radon presence in homes and radon prevention programs. In Illinois, she helped pass the Radon Awareness Act of 2008 and several other pieces of legislation. The Radon Awareness Act requires Illinois home sellers to provide a detailed disclosure form and education material on radon to homebuyers when a contract is signed.[3]

In Missouri, Linnertz has had less legislative success, though she has worked with lawmakers such as Jeanne Kirkton of Webster Groves and Sue Schoemehl of south St. Louis County to bring radon awareness to the Missouri statehouse. The legislature rejected a Missouri Radon Certification Program, a bill introduced by Schoemehl when she was in the House, which was designed to help residents detect radon in homes through testing. Missouri is also one of twenty-five states without Radon-Resistant New Construction Codes (RRNC).

CanSAR members pin Missouri's inaction on radon to a general lack of awareness of the problem in the state capital. Linnertz's own awareness of radon was raised after she lost her husband to lung cancer in 2006. A doctor first attributed his lung cancer to smoking, but her husband had not touched cigarettes in almost three decades. One month after he was diagnosed with lung cancer, Linnertz had her home tested for radon and found that the level was four times higher than the EPA's maximum standard of 4.0 picocuries per liter.[4]

Radon Awareness Legislation

Linnertz, who lives in Waterloo, Illinois, across the Mississippi River from the St. Louis area, has turned her sights farther east to Washington, D.C. She would like to see a federal law enacted to address the radon gas problem. Linnertz, who sits on the board of the American Association of Radon Scientists and Technologists, also would like to see the EPA lower the level deemed safe for radon exposure from 4.0 picocuries per liter to 3.0. The World Health Organization (WHO) has set its safe level at 2.7, according to Linnertz.[5]

Radon Gas Q & A

Jeanne Kirkton, a representative in the Missouri Legislature, answered the following questions about radon. She has a background in health care and focuses on health, mental health, and social services in the legislature.

Q. Is radon gas inhalation similar to smoking cigarettes in its effects? If you are a smoker, how does it increase your chances of developing cancer?

A. The radioactive particles formed in the breakdown of radon gas cause damage to chromosomes and the cells that line the lungs. When radon gas is inhaled, the broken down particles become stuck in the lungs and release damaging radioactive energy. Like radon gas, cigarette smoke can cause DNA damage and genetic mutation that alters the control of cell division. Exposure to cigarette smoke and radon gas compounds the risk of developing lung cancer.

Q. Is there a mythology, which pervades a lot of thinking of those who complain about "environmental alarmism," that if it is natural—it cannot be so bad? And, after all, radon is naturally occurring.

A. While the exact number of radon-related deaths may be disputed by some scientists, major health organizations, such as the Centers for Disease Control and Prevention, the American Lung Association, and the American Medical Association, all agree that radon causes thousands of preventable lung cancer deaths annually. Arguing that a naturally occurring compound cannot be harmful is specious. Many naturally occurring substances and events are potentially harmful or fatal given the right circumstance, dosage, or exposure.

Q. Are homes not usually radon-tested as part of home inspections before sales now? If you live in the same house for years, how often should you have it tested?

A. Homes should be tested if there is a change in living patterns that include the occupation of a lower level of your home. Even if the test results are below 4 pCi/L, the home should be tested again in the future. Buyers and sellers will often test for radon and a level of 4 pCi/L is used to determine if mitigation is necessary. Though testing is a good idea for long-term health protection, there are no laws in Missouri that require radon testing or radon mitigation by the seller.

Q. How expensive is a test? How expensive can it be to remedy a radon problem? Can you not just open up the basement windows and turn on a fan periodically?

A. The Missouri Department of Health will send a free radon test kit upon request. Other do-it-yourself kits generally run around ten dollars and charge an additional lab fee. Most do-it-yourself home tests utilize activated charcoal, which is inexpensive and relatively accurate (+/- 1 pCi/L), if the directions are followed carefully.

Notes

1. Staff Report, "Radon Fact Sheet" (Roanoke, Va.: Air Check, 2009), www.radon.com/radon/radon_facts.html.
2. EPA Radon Program, www.epa.gov/radon/states/missouri.html.
3. Gregorian, Cynthia Billhartz, "Radon Under the Radar," *St. Louis Post-Dispatch* (Jan. 17, 2013): B4.
4. French, Brittney, "Dangers of Radon," Community Reporting Class, Webster University (March 26, 2010).
5. Gregorian, B4.

Additional Readings

Committee on Health Risks of Exposure to Radon, "Health Effects of Exposure to Radon" (Washington, D.C.: National Academies Press, 1999).
Committee on Risk Assessment of Exposure to Radon in Drinking Water, "Risk Assessment of Radon in Drinking Water," (Washington, D.C.: National Academies Press, 1999).
Kladder, Douglas L., James F. Burkhart, and Steven R. Jelinek, *Protecting Your Home from Radon: A Step by Step Manual for Radon Reduction* (Colorado Springs: Colorado Vintage Companies, 1995).

Section 5
OTHER STATE
AND NATIONAL ISSUES

Photo by Courtney Martin

"Something will have gone out of us as a people if we ever let the remaining wilderness be destroyed; if we permit the last virgin forests to be turned into comic books and cigarette cases; if we drive the few remaining numbers of wild species into zoos or into extinction; if we pollute the last clean air and dirty the last clean streams and push our paved roads through the last of the silence, so that never again will Americans be free in their own country from the noise, the exhausts, the stinks . . ."
—Wallace Stegner,
"The Wilderness Letter," 1960

any, if not most, critical environmental problems cross state lines. They are national, if not global issues. This was brought home to me when writing an environmental story series in the 1980s. Shipments of highly radioactive debris from the nuclear disaster of 1979 at Three Mile Island (TMI) began traveling by rail through my St. Louis suburban town—just a few blocks from my own home. Protests began to erupt, not just in my area, but from Pennsylvania to Idaho along much of the length of the shipment route. A Gannett Foundation reporting grant allowed me to cover the protests from Harrisburg, Pennsylvania, to Idaho Falls, Idaho. Are these hazardous waste shipments a portent of things to come?

Of course, not all environmental issues are as dramatic as angry citizen protests over "mobile Chernobyls," as demonstrators called the nuclear rail shipments. Some of the topics covered in this section seem less urgent, such as light pollution or noise pollution or loss of local, state, and national park space. These issues may not be as disturbing as a potential nuclear waste accident or a coal ash spill, but they have much to do with our quality of life. If America ever gets as serious about a gross national happiness index as it is about the GNP (gross national product) index, then access to parks and freedom from noise and light pollution will have to figure heavily into any qualitative analysis that measures quality of life.

When taking an accounting of environmental issues that traverse state lines, phenomena that affect our food supply deserve prominent attention. What are the environmental impacts of genetically modified organisms as they are introduced into the crops that end up on our dinner table? What are the environmental consequences of the trend away from family farms to concentrated food operations? This section probes these questions, as well as concerns about species extinction.

Species extinction is an environmental issue that can affect our quality of life, our food supply, our very survival. The impending loss of aquatic animals known as Ozark hellbenders is a key indicator of the degradation of our water resources in Missouri. The mysterious decline in our honeybee populations is even more ominous, as their role in pollinating the fruits and vegetables we all love is critical. Fortunately, serious efforts are finally under way to find out what is going wrong with the "benders" and the bees—and it is about time.

RADIOACTIVE TRANSPORT

MOBILE CHERNOBYLS?

Photo by Don Corrigan

Transportation of hazardous waste across the country has always been a source of concern, but no dangerous cargo has sparked citizen anger like the radioactive rubble from the 1979 Three Mile Island nuclear plant meltdown. Organized protests sprang up across a multi-state area against the rail transport program to deliver radioactive debris from the Pennsylvania disaster site to a storage repository in Idaho. The shipments of highly radioactive waste caused many Americans to voice their opposition to the transports in Pennsylvania, Ohio, Indiana, Missouri, and states farther west.

In St. Louis, organized opposition was represented by the formation of a grassroots organization known as CART, or Citizens Against Radioactive Transport. Protesters in suburbs like Kirkwood and Webster Groves argued that the rail casks for damaged radioactive fuel rods were not dependable. They worried about train accidents and fires leading to cask ruptures and radioactive leaks. Some CART members argued that, at the very least, rail shipments should be routed through less-populated, more rural areas of the country.

The U.S. Department of Energy (DOE) and its contractors argued that the transport program was perfectly safe. However, there were problems with the more than twenty shipments between July 1986 and April 1990. In 1987, a TMI train hit a car stalled on the tracks in south St. Louis and gave the area a scare.[1] The shipments also were shut down for months after a buffer car to protect the cask rail car was discovered to be labeled as containing calcium carbide, a flammable chemical that can explode in a crash. That train, nevertheless, made it to an Idaho destination near Atomic City west of Idaho Falls.

A Dry Run for Yucca Mountain

Demonstrators from Pittsburgh to St. Louis were anxious about the shipments because they justifiably feared the TMI program was a dry run for Yucca Mountain, Nevada. The DOE had plans to ship millions of tons of spent nuclear fuel rods to a multi-billion dollar underground storage facility in Nevada.[2] The TMI shipments through the Midwest were seen as a pilot program to explore how extremely "hot" radioactive waste, stored temporarily at nuclear plants on the East Coast, could be transported to Yucca.

Marvin Resnikoff, a nuclear physicist and critic of nuclear power, said the TMI shipments and proposed Yucca shipments were all bad public policy: "The idea of putting all this spent fuel underground out West is a psychological thing. We all feel better if it is out of sight and buried, but the underground is not a perfect container. Especially when it needs to contain for 10,000 or 20,000 years.

"It is better stored in engineered facilities aboveground, on-site," added

Resnikoff. "But nuclear power plants do not want to think of themselves as waste management facilities, and Congress has done their dirty work by deciding to stick it all in the weakest state—in terms of political clout—of the union: Nevada."[3]

Nuke Shipment Plans Derailed

Missouri's CART members could rest a little easier about mass shipments of spent nuclear fuel rods traveling through their state after President Barack Obama canceled the proposed Yucca Mountain repository in 2011. The cancellation was a blow to nuclear industry hopes for ending storage of all spent fuel rods at plant locations.

Cancellation of Yucca was simply one piece of bad news for advocates of nuclear power. Proponents had hoped to tout nuclear as a clean energy fuel that does not produce air pollution or greenhouse gases. They had hoped for a "nuclear renaissance" after the hair-raising scares of the 1979 TMI disaster and the deadly 1986 Chernobyl nuclear plant disaster in Ukraine began to subside.

However, a 2011 nuclear plant disaster in Fukushima, Japan, caused renewed concern over nuclear safety. New fossil fuel discoveries also put a crimp in the economic viability of nuclear power in comparison. Finally, several new nuclear plants ordered in the United States—the first in three decades—were being plagued by construction delays in 2013 and budget overruns.[4]

Radioactive Transport Q & A

Kay Drey answers a few questions about the transport of radioactive materials. She is the cofounder of the Missouri Coalition for the Environment—a nonprofit that utilizes education, public engagement, and legal action in an effort to protect the environment.

Q. Nuclear power plants, which generate electricity, also produce spent fuel rods. Why is this material so radioactive and what dangers does it pose?

A. Spent fuel rods are removed from a nuclear power plant's reactor vessel after the rods have been fissioning for about three years. They are dangerously radioactive and are described as "high-level waste." No safe location exists for the temporary storage or permanent location of commercial irradiated rods.

Q. What is the solution to all the spent fuel rods at plants now? Are they vulnerable to terrorism if they are not removed and shipped to one location where they can be isolated and protected?

A. Fuel rods should not be kept crowded in fuel pools at nuclear power plants, as they are now. A somewhat safer, temporary storage solution is to store the rods in concrete casks on-site at each nuclear power plant. They must be kept in a guarded location, under constant surveillance. Irradiated fuel rods are always vulnerable to acts of terrorism, fire, and accidents.

Q. Nuclear power has been touted as green energy that is cleaner than fossil fuels and that will address concerns about global warming. Is the verdict still out on this proposition?

A. During the construction of the nuclear power plants and the creation of the uranium fuel rods—during the mining, milling, chemical conversion, and enrichment of the uranium, and the fabrication of the rods—carbon dioxide is released. The public is not generally informed that every nuclear power plant releases radioactive gases, liquids, and particles into the air and into the lake, ocean, or river that provides the plant's cooling water—as a part of the routine operation of the plant. It does not take an accident for release of radioactivity.

Q. Missouri may be the site for the manufacture of a new generation of smaller, mobile, less costly nuclear power generators. Are these likely to be cleaner—with fewer fuel disposal problems—than plants like Callaway in Missouri or Braidwood in Illinois?

A. The proposed "small modular reactors" would pose the same range of potential accidents, expose plant workers to inhumane levels of radiation, and generate long-lived, highly radioactive fuel and other radioactive parts and components for which no safe, permanent disposal site may ever be found.

Notes

1. Corrigan, Don, "TMI Shipments Extended Into 1989," *Webster-Kirkwood Times* (Nov. 11, 1988): 5-6.
2. Corrigan, Don, "TMI Shipment Protesters: From Pennsylvania to Idaho, They're Protesting," *Webster-Kirkwood Times* (Nov. 25, 1988): 5.
3. Corrigan, Don, "TMI Shipments Are Tip of a Nuclear Iceberg," *Webster-Kirkwood Times* (Dec. 16, 1988): 5, 10.
4. Mann, Charles G., "The Conversation: Responses and Reverberations," *The Atlantic* (July–August 2013): 14.

Additional Readings

Morris, Robert, *Environmental Case for Nuclear Power: Economic, Medical, and Political Considerations* (St. Paul, Minn: Paragon House, 2000).
Osif, Bonnie, *TMI 25 Years Later: The Three Mile Island Nuclear Power Plant Accident and Its Impact* (University Park: Pennsylvania State University Press, 2004).
Rosen, Ira, and Mike Gray, *The Warning: Accident at Three Mile Island: A Nuclear Omen for the Age of Terror* (New York: W. W. Norton & Company, reissue edition, 2003).
Walker, Samuel J., *Three Mile Island: A Nuclear Crisis in Historical Perspective* (Berkeley: University of California Press, 2004).

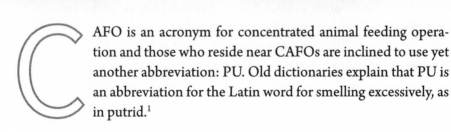

CAFOs
CAN YOU SMELL THAT SMELL?

Photo by
Courtney Martin

C AFO is an acronym for concentrated animal feeding operation and those who reside near CAFOs are inclined to use yet another abbreviation: PU. Old dictionaries explain that PU is an abbreviation for the Latin word for smelling excessively, as in putrid.[1]

For more than a decade in Missouri, newspapers have been covering the rise of CAFOs, and the resulting increase in putrid smells. State legislators have even introduced bills forbidding new CAFOS from being built within five miles of a state park or historic landmark.[2]

The stench of a large factory hog farm can be more than just a nauseating nuisance. *Science Now* and other publications have reported on studies detailing the potential for a noxious mix of farm emissions, which can include hydrogen sulfide, ammonia, allergens, and particulates. Research now shows that CAFO emissions can cause quantifiable increases in stress and fatigue with measurable hikes in blood pressure and blood sugar levels.[3] The University of North Carolina, the Purdue University Extension Service, and other academic institutions have studied the odor issue of CAFOs.

Industrial-scale farms can have a considerable number of adverse environmental impacts on the air, water, and land. Most of these effects stem from the massive quantities of animal waste, which is often collected in open pits. A Purdue study, "CAFOs and Public Health: Odor and Its Possible Health Effects," argues that much more attention has to be given to odor abatement, proper setbacks, proper manure management with biofilters, and composting.[4]

It Is Not Just the Smell

For groups like the Missouri Farmers Union (MFU), Missouri Coalition for the Environment (MCE), Missouri Rural Crisis Center (MRCC), and Missouri Votes Conservation (MVC), the problem with CAFOs is not just the smell. These groups have lamented the loss of family farms and the decline of rural main streets as large corporations take over agriculture and local economies. They have also focused on concerns about CAFOs raising animals pumped with antibiotics and hormones, as well as what happens to humans who consume meat produced from these animals.

Kathleen Logan Smith of MCE contends that there is a direct link between the chemicals used by factory farms and hikes in antibiotic-resistant diseases affecting rural Missourians. She also sees a connection between hormone injections and stillbirths in livestock. MCE and MVC have both raised concerns about chemicals used by CAFOs ending up in our water and food supply.[5]

Urban residents in Missouri and across the United States are being sensitized to potential problems with CAFOs due to documentary makers shining a spotlight on agriculture. Among the most cited offerings: "Farming Was My Life: The Hidden Costs of CAFOs," a series on YouTube, which hits close to home with the situation in Missouri; *Pig Business: The True Cost of Cheap Meat*, which looks at the health and economic impacts of CAFOs; and, *Food Inc.*, a film that examines the industrial production of chicken, beef, and pork.

No Middle Ground on CAFOs

Perhaps it is no surprise that such companies as Monsanto, Tyson Foods, Smithfield Foods, and Perdue Farms have offered rebuttals to the critiques of the modern food industry. An alliance of food production companies, spearheaded by the American Meat Institute, has created a website, SafeFoodInc.org, to respond to the claims made in the film *Food Inc.* Companies argue that global agricultural operations are best suited to affordably feed the world. According to John Ikerd, a professor emeritus of agricultural economics at the University of Missouri–Columbia, one thing promoters and opponents of CAFOs can agree on: there is more conflict ahead. Writes Ikerd: "CAFO promoters accuse opponents of being emotional, uninformed radicals, opposed to modern agriculture and to progress in general. Opponents accuse CAFO promoters of being insensitive, self-seeking bullies, unconcerned about the rights of other people in the community."[6]

CAFOs Q & A

Tim Gibbons answers a few questions about CAFOs. He works with the Missouri Rural Crisis Center (MRCC). MRCC, a statewide farm and rural membership organization, has a twenty-eight-year history of fighting for independent family farms and rural communities and their economies.

Q. Concentrated animal feeding operations (CAFOs) are sometimes called factory farms. How do these change the agricultural landscape?

A. A CAFO is technically classified as a livestock operation with more than a thousand animal units—animal units are defined differently for different species—that houses livestock in a concentrated manner. For the past few decades, multinational meatpackers have systematically put family farm livestock operations out of business. As an example, since 1985, nearly 90 percent of hog operations in Missouri have gone out of business, from 23,000 operations in 1985 to around 3,000 today. This has not only been damaging to farm families, but also the rural communities in which they live.

Q. How is meat production now dominated by CAFOs?

A. Nearly 70 percent of U.S. hog slaughter is controlled by four agribusiness giants—Smithfield Foods, Cargill, Tyson Foods, and JBS/Swift. And 80 to 90 percent of cattle slaughter is controlled by four meatpackers—JBS/Swift, Cargill, Tyson Foods, and National Beef. The implications of this monopolized marketplace—i.e., a few multinational meatpackers controlling our food supply—has been extremely damaging to markets, farm families, and rural economies and communities.

Q. CAFO companies argue that their big operations are needed to feed an expanding world population.

A. Yes, they do argue that, often. The problem is that it is not true. Family farm livestock operations are the most efficient producers of livestock. One of the central problems is that we do not have a free, open, and competitive marketplace. Instead, we have a marketplace that is controlled by concentration, vertical integration, and monopolization. This type of market control has given a few multibillion-dollar meatpackers an inordinate amount of power—and this power was and is used to create excessive market share and market control for themselves at the expense of independent livestock producers. These meatpackers consistently report record quarterly profits, while the rural economy suffers, while independent livestock producers work harder for less and have increasingly limited options in the raising and selling of livestock, while consumers pay more and more at the grocery store.

Notes

1. Smart Aleck's Guide: Playground Jungle, "What Does P.U. Stand For?" www.playgroundjungle.com/2010/08/what-does-pu-stand-for.html.
2. Hotflash Blog, "A Smell That Could Buckle Your Knees: CAFOs Should Be Locally Controlled," blog.showmeprogress.com/showDiary.do?diaryId=738.
3. Adams, Jill, "Hog Farm Stink Raises Neighbor's Blood Pressure," *Science Now* (Nov. 7, 2012): 1-3.
4. Ebner, Paul, "CAFOs and Public Health: Odor and Its Possible Health Effects," *Purdue University Agricultural Extension Studies* (March, 2008): 1–3.
5. Fitz, Don, "Sustainable Animal Raising vs. CAFOs," *The Healthy Planet* (Jan. 2012): 13.
6. Ikerd, John, "CAFOs vs. Rural Communities," *In Motion Magazine* (Sept. 15, 2008): 1-3. See: www.inmotionmagazine.com/ra08/ikerd_cafo08.html.

Additional Readings

Berry, Wendell, *Bringing It to the Table* (Berkeley, Calif.: Counterpoint Press, 2009).
Imhoff, Daniel, *The Tragedy of Industrial Animal Factories* (San Rafael, Calif.: Insight Editions, 2010).
Kirby, David, *Animal Factory: The Looming Threat of Industrial Pig, Dairy, and Poultry Farms to Humans and the Environment* (New York: St. Martin's Press, 2010).
Midkiff, Ken and Wendell Berry, *The Meat You Eat: How Corporate Farming Has Endangered America's Food Supply* (New York: St. Martin's Griffin, 2005).

GMOs AND LABELING
A FOOD FIGHT

Plant science sounds like a complex topic tailor-made to bore all
but a few highly credentialed experts. The idea of discussing the
science of plants may make most people nod off, but things can
get pretty noisy when the issue becomes genetically modified
organisms (GMOs). The controversy over GMOs has raged in
Europe for several decades, and in recent years, many Americans have been
drawn into the debate.

St. Louis has become a focal point for much of that debate in America and globally. That is because the world's largest researcher, developer, and producer of GMOs, the Monsanto Company, is headquartered in St. Louis. At the same time Monsanto vigorously defends its GMO operations, the number of its critics located in the Gateway City has been growing, with the rise of groups such as the Organic Consumers Association, Institute for Responsible Technology, Non-GMO Project, and the Gateway Green Alliance.

The basic argument against GMOs holds that they are not natural and that GMO products are derived through dangerous meddling with biological processes that have taken eons to evolve.[1] GMO critics describe genetically modified foods as "Frankenfoods" that could have unintended toxic and allergic consequences. In addition to health concerns, critics also contend that GMOs have powerful economic and environmental consequences that are only now coming into view.[2]

What Is a GMO?

GMO foods, including certain strains of corn, soybeans, fruits, vegetables, and even fish, have their origin in the laboratory where scientists alter the food's genetic makeup. This may be done to make them more resistant to pests or to help them withstand climate adversity ranging from intense cold to drought. Sometimes the goal is to make the edible results more consistent and more nutritious. The science involves recombinant DNA technology using DNA molecules from different sources to design a new set of genes.[3]

Proponents of GMOs cite studies showing their positive impact in the farm field and on the dinner table. They also contend that the use of genetically modified foods can address the expanding demand for food as world population grows. Detractors cite studies that show ill effects from GMO foods, ranging from allergic reactions to organ failure. Reliable, long-term data on GMOs and their health effects are hard to ascertain, which may be why the controversy continues.[4]

One aspect of the GMO debate involves labeling: should foods produced through GMO technology be labeled as such, so Americans can make up their own minds whether to purchase and consume such products? U.S. Senator Bernie Sanders (I-Vermont) posed the question this way: "In the U.S., food labels must already list more than 3,000 ingredients ranging from gluten, aspartame, high-fructose corn syrup, trans-fats or MSG—but not genetically altered ingredients. Around the world, by contrast, forty-nine countries require labels on foods that contain genetically engineered ingredients."[5]

GMO Labeling Battle Rages

Members of the St. Louis Gateway Green Alliance and Safe Food Action St. Louis demonstrated against GMOs in 2012, in part to show solidarity with the "Just Label It Campaign" in California. Supporters of labeling GMOs sponsored Proposition 37 on the California ballot that would require labeling genetically modified foods. However, California voters rejected the ballot proposition in November 2012.

Supporters of the "Label It" proposition blamed their defeat on millions of dollars spent by food corporations and agricultural biotechnology companies to defeat it. Opponents of Prop 37 said it violated the First Amendment by mandating commercial speech. They also contended that it would increase food costs for Americans, and would only enrich anti-biotech activists and their lawyers.

GMOs Q & A

Barbara Ann Chicherio has worked on environmental and social justice projects for the past twenty-five years. She has worked in state mental hospitals and in schools with children with social, emotional, and behavior concerns.

Q. What is a genetically modified organism (GMO) and what does it have to do with genetically modified foods?

A. GMOs are plants or animals created through the gene splicing techniques of biotechnology—also called genetic engineering or GE. This experimental technology merges DNA from different species, creating unstable combinations of plant, animal, bacterial, and viral genes that cannot occur in nature or in traditional crossbreeding.

Q. What are some examples of genetically modified crops or foodstuffs that have become part of the array of products on grocery shelves?

A. GMO plants—that are now most commonly found in foods—are corn and soy. About 85 percent of soy grown in the United States is genetically modified and soy is found in many processed foods. While GE sweet corn is not yet on the market, common field corn is now about 90 percent genetically engineered. This corn is fed to cattle raised for human consumption, it is used to make corn syrup (which is found in many foods), and it is used in ethanol.

Q. GMOs and genetically engineered foods are regulated by U.S. agencies such as the USDA, FDA, and EPA. What kinds of regulations have these agencies considered?

A. During the Reagan administration the White House issued a policy document— "Coordinated Framework for the Regulation of Biotechnology"—directed at preventing Congress from getting involved in the debate for the regulation of GMOs. Addressed to the three relevant regulatory agencies—FDA, EPA, and USDA—the directive provided that products derived from biotechnology would be regulated within the framework of already existing laws. So GMOs did not require special treatment and would be subject to the same system of approval as non-transgenic products.

Q. Are the major objections to GMOS by some environmentalists focused on the potential failure of modern science to anticipate some of the negative outcomes of genetic-engineering experiments?

A. Unintended outcomes are just one of the many concerns that environmentalists have regarding GMOs. As you may be aware, Monsanto's Round Up Ready soybeans are genetically engineered to be pesticide resistant to Monsanto's product, Round Up. Monsanto sells its Round Up Ready soybeans with Round Up (glyphosate), as a package. Since its inception, environmentalists have been concerned that the overuse of glyphosate would lead to pesticide tolerance and the growth of "super weeds." This concern has become a reality and now farmers are using glyphosate along with the old-line pesticides to combat these resistant weeds.

Notes

1. Bakshi, A., "Potential Adverse Health Effects of Genetically Modified Crops," *Journal of Toxicology and Environmental Health* (2003, Part B, 6): 211-225.
2. Sesana, Laura, "Frankenfoods: The Debate Over Genetically Modified Foods," *The Washington Times* (April 15, 2013): 1-3.
3. Johnson, S. A., and D. C. Tang, "Gene Gun Transfection of Animal Cells and Genetic Immunization," *Methods in Cell Biology* (1994): 253-365.
4. Sesana, 3-7.
5. Abrams, Brett, "Food Democracy Now Urges Senators to Pass Bill Allowing States To Label Genetically Modified Foods," *Fitzgibbon Media Release* (June 21, 2012): 1-2.

Additional Readings

Fedoroff, Nina V., and Nancy Marie Brown, *Mendel in the Kitchen: A Scientist's View of Genetically Modified Food* (Washington, D.C.: Joseph Henry Press, 2006).
Ruse, Michael, *Genetically Modified Foods: Debating Biotechnology* (New York: Prometheus Books, 2002).
Schurman, Rachel, and William Munro, *Fighting for the Future of Food: Activists Versus Agribusiness in the Struggle Over Biotechnology* (St. Paul: University of Minnesota Press, 2010).
Weasel, Lisa H., *Inside the Controversy Over Genetically Modified Food* (New York: AMACOM Publishers, 2008).

POLLINATORS KAPUT
COLONIES COLLAPSING

olony collapse disorder (CCD) is the description for the alarming loss of honeybee colonies in North America, a phenomenon first tagged as CCD in about 2006.[1] Quite simply, the honeybees are disappearing. The loss is alarming to both scientists and beekeepers because so many agricultural crops are pollinated by bees. However, it is hardly just a farming issue or an economic matter; the loss raises red flags for ecology and the environment, as bees are essential to reproduction of plant life in the wild.

The bees are disappearing, but one place where they can still be found is at the bee exhibit at Powder Valley Nature Center located near the intersection of I-44 and I-270 in Kirkwood. Ted Jansen, who tended the Powder Valley bee exhibit when it was first installed in the early 1990s, has watched the feral bee population dwindle in recent years. A member of the Eastern Missouri Beekeeping Association, Jansen has had close to a hundred honeybee colonies on his own property in Chesterfield and has been raising them for years.

"I think we are in trouble with the honeybee," says Jansen. "There are so many chemicals and pesticides being used. There are very few bees for pollination left in the wild."[2] The North American Pollinator Protection Campaign (NAPPC) agrees with Jansen, who is known as the "bee whisperer" because of his obvious affection for the species. The NAPPC attributes colony collapse disorder to a number of factors, such as habitat destruction, invasive mites, improper use of pesticides, and global warming.[3]

Plight of the Honeybees

Many beekeepers, such as Jansen, blame a lot of the bees' problems on the parasitic Varroa mite, which sucks fluids from the circulatory system. However, scientists note that mite infestations usually result in thousands of dead bees in a pile in front of their hives. With what is going on now, bees are disappearing without a trace.[4]

Some environmentalists blame the bee losses on Monsanto's genetically engineered crops such as Bt corn. Their contention is that a toxin incorporated in the corn to kill insects is being absorbed by the bees and provokes an immune response in the bees that prevents proper memory function. The resulting confusion impairs navigational ability and the bees are unable to find their way back to their hives.[5] Absorption or ingestion of the toxin is also said to reduce the bees' ability to survive the presence of parasites such as Varroa mites.

Monsanto has been the target of criticism not only within the United States but all over the world. In response, Monsanto formed a Honey Bee

Advisory Council in 2013 and rolled out its Honey Bee Health Page on its website at a three-day bee research summit in Chesterfield.[6] Monsanto has also invested in honeybee research and, according to the *St. Louis Business Journal*, in 2011 acquired Beelogics, a startup company founded in 2007 to find biological tools for addressing the diseases affecting bees.

Pollinator Weeks, Pollinator Dinners

To sensitize the general public to the plight of the honeybees, the St. Louis Zoo has offered National Pollinator Week activities in June and special pollinator dinners with honey tastings and guest speakers talking about ways humans can help honeybees. The St. Louis Zoo WildCare Institute Center for Native Pollinator Conservation focuses on the importance of native pollinators for the survival of wildlife, ecosystems, and agriculture.

The St. Louis Zoo has also been pivotal in the PAUSE (Pollinators/ Art/Urban Agriculture/Society/and the Environment) program to encourage college students to address what has become a world crisis of declining bee populations. Ed Spevak, a PAUSE mentor and curator of invertebrates at the zoo, insists that everyone can help the bees "by growing a wildflower garden, protecting habitat, and reducing our use of pesticides and herbicides."[7]

Bees Q&A

Tom Van Arsdall answers a few questions about disappearing bees. He is the public affairs director at Pollinator Partnership (P2) and represents P2 in the national policy arena. P2 (www.pollinator.org) is a nonprofit whose mission is to catalyze stewardship of biodiversity.

Q. Is it an exaggeration to say that one out of every three bites of food that we eat depends on pollinators such as honeybees or bumblebees? Does that explain the alarm over colony collapse disorder?

A. The "one out of every three bites of food" is an often-used phrase to characterize the importance of insect/animal pollination to our food supply, not just in the United States, but worldwide. And it is not just bees—it is all pollinators. The alarm over CCD is that managed honeybees have long been the workhorse in providing ag pollination services.

Q. Honeybees are a big part of our plant ecology in America. Is colony collapse disorder affecting the ecology of the plant world in other parts of the globe?

A. There are documented honeybee die-offs in Europe, but it is unclear whether it is the same as CCD in the United States. Worldwide, honeybee populations appear to be stable, not impacted by whatever is happening. Worldwide, loss of native pollinators due to loss of habitat and other factors appears to be a growing problem of serious concern.

Q. What crops, fruits and vegetables, will suffer most if colony collapse disorder worsens in the United States and around the world?

A. Most of the major acreage crops, such as maize, wheat, and corn, are wind-pollinated. However, the majority of fruits, vegetables, and nuts are insect/animal pollinated. Important forage crops, such as clovers, are also bee pollinated, as are many of the oilseed crops. The world would not go hungry in a calorie sense, but our diet would be bland, and deficient in many of the vitamins and micronutrients that are required for good health and nutrition.

Q. Is there something local home owners, conservationists, and environmentalists can do to bring back the bee populations and counteract colony collapse disorder?

A. Yes! Plant for pollinators, share our landscapes, and when using pesticides do so in ways that minimize the impact on pollinators.

Notes

1. Pennsylvania State University of Agricultural Sciences, "Honey Bee Die-off Alarms Beekeepers, Crop Growers and Researchers," Jan. 29, 2007, www.aginfo.psu.edu/News?07Jan/Honey-Bees.htm.
2. Mannino, Fran, "Colony Collapse Disorder," *Webster-Kirkwood Times* (June 29, 2007): 1.
3. Ibid.
4. Cain, Sarah, "The Bees Are Dying," *The Health Wyze Report* (October, 2010): 1-5.
5. Ibid.
6. Solomont, E.B., "Monsanto Launches Honeybee Advisory Council," *St. Louis Business Journal* (June 14, 2013), www.bizjournals.com/stlouis/news/2013/06/14/monsanto-launches-honey-bee-advisory.html.
7. Saint Louis Zoo, "National Pollinators Week Is June 18-24," press release (June 11, 2012): 2-3.

Additional Readings

Bishop, Holly, *Robbing the Bees: A Biography of Honey* (New York: Atria Press, 2006).

Jacobsen, Rowen, *Fruitless Fall: The Collapse of the Honey Bee and the Coming Agricultural Crisis* (New York: Bloomsbury Press, 2009).

Schacker, Michael, *A Spring Without Bees: How Colony Collapse Disorder Has Endangered Our Food Supply* (New York: Lyons Press, 2009).

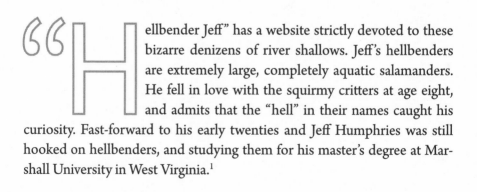

HELLBENDERS
ENDANGERED
SPECIES

"Hellbender Jeff" has a website strictly devoted to these bizarre denizens of river shallows. Jeff's hellbenders are extremely large, completely aquatic salamanders. He fell in love with the squirmy critters at age eight, and admits that the "hell" in their names caught his curiosity. Fast-forward to his early twenties and Jeff Humphries was still hooked on hellbenders, and studying them for his master's degree at Marshall University in West Virginia.[1]

Now employed with the North Carolina Wildlife Resources Commission Wildlife Diversity Program, Humphries is concerned that these slippery fellows, who have survived a hundred million years on the planet, are now endangered because of human activity. Eastern hellbenders, for the most part, are found in streams in the Appalachians and Ohio River Valley. Ozark hellbenders in the Missouri Ozarks are in trouble, as only about four hundred are thought to be left in the rivers and tributaries of the Ozark Scenic Riverways.[2]

Like so many animal species whose survival is under threat, hellbenders have been having problems because of habitat degradation. This includes water pollution that could be interfering with their reproduction, general decline in water quality with loss of oxygen, erosion issues and silt covering the rocky places where hellbenders like to live and produce their young.

Even before humans defiled their environment, hellbenders had to deal with hostility from *Homo sapiens*. They were viewed as monsters and stakes were driven through them. Fishermen killed them because they thought they hurt trout and bass fishing. For a time, they were captured by the pet trade for commercial sale.

Heaven-Sent Help for Hellbenders

Extinction for Ozark hellbenders could happen within several decades without intervention, but there is some good news. St. Louis Zoo experts are intervening, and hellbenders may get a new lease on life. Interestingly enough, another Jeff has taken an interest in the unusual salamanders. Jeff Ettling, curator of herpetology and aquatics at the zoo, has been working to bring back their population with a hellbender breeding project. Ettling and his zoo colleagues have found success with the creation of an artificial stream.

"We have created an artificial, indoor stream that is three feet wide, eighteen inches deep and eighty-five feet long in the basement of the Herpetarium," Ettling said. "We keep it at fifty-five degrees and we have even created mists at times to make it rain and to duplicate the rain events of the Ozarks. After months and months without success, we finally had our first successful breeding of hellbenders on October 8, 2011."[3]

More than 3,900 Ozark hellbenders are thriving in the artificial stream at the zoo, according to Ettling. The challenge now is to reintroduce them to native Ozark habitat such as the Current, Jacks Fork, and Eleven Point rivers. That challenge includes identifying the habitat issues that have caused survival problems for the creatures. One of the projects under way at the zoo is to create artificial, concrete nesting boxes for the hellbenders. These would substitute for rock habitats that have been silted over and might also be useful for the creatures to hide in at night.

Praise for Zoo's Hellbender Effort

The St. Louis Zoo is getting praise from all over the country for its work with hellbenders, including from North Carolina's "Hellbender Jeff." He describes the success of the zoo with its captive breeding as "huge," but adds, "The big question is: 'How do you restore populations of hellbenders if their habitat is still polluted?' Ideally, we should restore the health of the rivers and then restock the hellbenders."[4]

Two conservation groups filed notice in 2013 that they will sue the U.S. Forest Service and the U.S. Fish and Wildlife Service for poor management of waterway areas in which Ozark hellbenders live in Missouri. The Endangered Species Act allows for such lawsuits against the government. Environmental groups see the lawsuits as a way to nudge the government into action to protect wildlife. And they argue that hellbenders' problems are an indication of what is happening to water quality in Missouri.[5]

Hellbenders Q & A

Jeff Humphries answers a few questions about hellbenders and their population decline. He is currently a wildlife diversity biologist with the North Carolina Wildlife Resources Commission.

Q. Are hellbenders not like the proverbial "canary in the coal mine," because their health problems indicate that our streams are polluted and sickly?

A. I oftentimes think that hellbenders are much better indicators of the health of streams than the indicators biologists usually use, like aquatic invertebrates or fish. In most of the hellbender's range, if a stream looks really healthy (clear water, a lot of rocks, and not much siltation), it is easy to find a lot of hellbenders. In short, if hellbenders are doing well in a river, the river is doing well as a whole.

Q. What environmental impacts have been toughest on hellbenders?

A. There are certainly many things that have impacted hellbender populations—including dams, urbanization, sewage and toxic discharges from towns and cities, coal mining effects, collection for the pet trade, and unknown causes—but sedimentation from the removal of forested buffers is certainly one of the big factors. Rivers in the eastern United States, where hellbenders used to exist, were naturally buffered from sediment runoff by forests. When that forest buffer is taken away, and replaced by agriculture, sediment flows directly into streams and rivers and covers up the rocky habitat that hellbenders need to survive.

Q. How is the population of hellbenders declining in Missouri and what are some of the signs of a decline in the health of the hellbenders?

A. It is important to note that the reasons for declines in your part of the country are somewhat unknown. However, Missouri populations are showing signs of strange abnormalities and lesions on their bodies, low sperm counts, and very little breeding despite the streams still appearing to be fairly healthy. Biologists at the Missouri Department of Conservation are working hard to find out why this is happening. Something beyond sedimentation from agriculture appears to be causing hellbender declines in the Missouri region.

Q. Hellbenders breathe entirely through their skin, so is this another reason they are especially sensitive to changes in the makeup of the water in which they live?

A. Sure. All amphibians are sensitive to toxins or other things we throw at them because they have permeable skin that pretty much takes up whatever is in their environment very quickly. However, hellbenders have more of a problem because they are very specialized—and they do not leave the water. They need very clean, very clear, very rocky habitat to survive.

Notes

1. Humphries, Jeff, "What's a Hellbender?" The Hellbender Homepage, www.hellbenders.org/The_Hellbender_Homepage/Home.html.
2. Corrigan, Don, "Ozark Hellbender," *Webster-Kirkwood Times* (March 22, 2013): 12A-13A.
3. Ibid.
4. Ibid.
5. Ibid.

Additional Readings

Coatney Jr., C.E., "Home Range and Nocturnal Activity of the Ozark Hellbender," Unpublished Thesis (Springfield: Southeast Missouri State University, 1982).
Humphries, W. J., "Ecology and Population Demography of the Hellbender," Thesis (Huntington, W.V.: Marshall University, 1999).
Swanson, P. L., "Notes on the Amphibians and Reptiles of Venango County, Pennsylvania," *The American Naturalist* 40 (1948).

POWER TO THE
PARKS PEOPLE

P arks in Missouri are one of the outdoor environmental success stories in the Show-Me State. At the same time, parks always seem to be on the chopping block when it comes to budget-cutting, whether at the local, state, or national level. This is quite disconcerting, because parks are an essential part of a sustainable lifestyle. They provide sustenance for the heart and the soul, but only eternal vigilance protects parks for the people.

For a gem called Forest Park in St. Louis, much of that eternal vigilance comes from Forest Park Forever, a nonprofit group that has saved parcels of the park from development, and promoted access, recreation, infrastructure—and memories. "I have so many good memories of Forest Park—it is hard to choose just one," declared Joe Edwards, founder of Blueberry Hill in University City. "I got to ride a female elephant—at the park's zoo—interestingly named 'Big Jim,' and I laughed when the gorillas splashed water on visitors, who actually loved it."[1]

Edwards was responding to the campaign known as 50,000 Days in Forest Park: Which Was Your Favorite? The ongoing campaign was to celebrate a major milestone: the 50,000th day since Forest Park's establishment on June 24, 1876.[2] A project of Forest Park Forever, the campaign elicited thousands of comments like the one from Edwards, who is known as the King of Blueberry Hill in St. Louis.

Parks Are for the People

Missouri is a sadly divided state on many political issues, but if there is one thing St. Louis and Missouri residents agree on—it is that parks are a priority. Do not mess with our parks, make them better!

The St. Louis Gateway Arch, an internationally recognized symbol, is anchored in the riverfront national park known as the Jefferson National Expansion Memorial. As the arch was approaching its fiftieth birthday in 2015, it was showing signs of corrosion and decay. The same could be said of the park grounds, which were in need of renewal and better access for the host city, St. Louis. Voters came to the rescue in April 2013 when they passed Proposition P, promoted by the grassroots Citizens for Safe and Public Parks Initiative.[3]

Critics understandably objected that the federal government should take care of the arch and its grounds, not local taxpayers, since it is a national park. However, given the budget fights in Washington, D.C., it could be a long time before the National Park Service was funded to care for and repair the arch area. Budget bungling in the nation's capital has already hurt other national park areas in Missouri. The Ozark Riverways have endured cuts from the U.S. Congress's "sequester," which translate into reduced staffing, park hours, refuse services and upkeep, never mind new acquisitions.[4]

State Parks Also Suffer

State parks have also suffered. Due to decades of deferred funding, they need $400 million in critical infrastructure repairs, from aging sewer and electrical systems to the bridges and culverts that support the Katy Trail. Missouri outdoor and environmental groups have been making noise about all this. And they have caught the attention of legislators, who seem to know that taking care of parks is not a partisan issue.

If anyone doubts Missouri's love affair with parks, they might want to recall the furor triggered in 2011 when St. Louis County Executive Charlie Dooley proposed closing twenty county parks. Dooley said the closings were necessary to address a budget running in the red. Hundreds of county residents turned out at public hearings and rallies to save the parks. Hikers, bikers, runners, anglers, kayakers, and environmental groups ranging from the Coalition for the Environment and the Open Space Council to Environment Missouri got in on the action. The county parks were saved, proving: Parks are for the people![5]

Save the Parks Q & A

Sue Gustafson agreed to answer a few questions about parks. She has served as vice president of conservation for the St. Louis Audubon Society, president of the Webster Groves Nature Study Society, and president of the Audubon Society of Missouri.

Q. Why is the save the parks movement really an environmental issue? How do parks figure into the history and tradition of the environmental movement in America?

A. It is an environmental issue because it involves the preservation of open spaces and the quality of land, water, and even air. The establishment of the first national parks and wildlife refuges gave confirmation that special areas needed to be protected in an age of ever-increasing "progress"—industrialization/urbanization.

Q. What kinds of recreational activities make sense in our parks, and what kinds of activities should be outlawed in order to preserve our natural spaces?

A. Since these areas are public, there needs to be a balance between "active" recreational opportunities—such as soccer fields—and "passive" activities, such as wildlife viewing/hiking trails. Active opportunities that severely compromise habitat and/or cause public nuisance to other park attendees, such as widespread ATV usage, should be extremely limited.

Q. As funding runs dry and budgets get tight, some government officials target local or state or national parks for cuts as a way to balance the books. How widespread has this phenomenon been?

A. It has been common at the federal level for quite some time, especially in periods of recession and economic downturn. Management of state parks has followed suit, but it only seems recently that county and city parks are falling victim to budget cuts, but it is probably because such jurisdictions have had better balanced budgets historically.

Q. Can parks suffer a bit of benign neglect and then be given some TLC when budgets improve without a lot of long-term harm being done?

A. If habitat management is neglected, one of the most detrimental consequences is the explosion of invasive species that can quickly result in the loss of native species. In the long run, it will cost more to eradicate the invasives in order to restore the natives than it would have cost to properly manage the habitat originally.

Notes

1. Hulsey, Molly, "50,000 Days in Forest Park: Which Was Your Favorite," FleishmanHillard Brand Marketing Release (May 13, 2013): 1-3.
2. Ibid.
3. Mowers, Jaime, "Prop P Passes For Arch, Parks & Trails," *West End Word* (April 9, 2013): 4.
4. Schaper, Jo, "Sequester Hits Riverways Hard; Lakes Hurt Less," *River Hills Traveler* (St. Clair, Mo., May 1, 2013): 1.
5. Corrigan, Don, "Groups Mobilize to Halt Closing of County Parks," *South County Times* (Nov. 18, 2011): 1. See also: www.southcountytimes.com/articles-features-i-2011-11-18.

Additional Readings

Duncan, Dayton and Ken Burns, *The National Parks: America's Best Idea* (New York: Random House, 2009).
Flader, Susan, *Exploring Missouri's Legacy: State Parks and Historic Sites* (Columbia: University of Missouri Press, 1992).
Harris, NiNi, and Esley Hamilton, *St. Louis Parks* (St. Louis: Reedy Press, 2012).

SPIN IT TO WIN IT!

EARN ENTRIES NOW!
Grand Finale March 30, 2013
Win up to
$1,000,000

LUMIÈRE PLACE
Casino & Hotel

Entries spend at Lumière Place and ask for Lumière Place Player Rewards.

See myChoice® Center for details.

Light Pollution
WHEN STARS DON'T TWINKLE

A larming examples of water pollution, air pollution, and even noise pollution are not so hard to find in Missouri, but how about light pollution? Can Missouri really be classified as a light polluter? After all, Missouri's urban centers have nothing to compare to the glare of Times Square in New York City, the glitz of an illuminated Los Angeles night sky, or the lights of the Las Vegas Strip. Nevertheless, the bright lights of the metro areas of St. Louis and Kansas City are easy to spot on satellite reconnaissance photos.

Some Missouri residents do feel that the state needs to address the issue of excessive and non-essential light, not just in urban areas, but also in state parks where folks go to get away from the glow. Two lawmakers in the state's 2009 legislative session were moved to introduce bills to reduce light in state parks, wilderness areas, and military training facilities. The legislation's goal was to reduce light to no more than twice the natural brightness of the night sky by 2025.[1]

Rep. Jason Holsman (D-Kansas City) told the Associated Press that his bill would increase awareness of the idea of light pollution, while giving outdoor enthusiasts a better look at the Milky Way on their camping trips. Sen. Joan Bray (D-University City) agreed with Holsman that it was time to address the issue of the continuing aesthetic decline of night skies in the state.[2]

Not Just an Aesthetic Concern

Three Missouri State University professors argue that the issue of obtrusive artificial light is not just an aesthetic concern. Extravagant and misdirected light from streetlights, residences, and commercial properties is not simply an ugly annoyance, but also affects the health of humans and wildlife, as well as wasting energy. In their study, "The Economics of Global Light Pollution," professors Terrel Gallaway, Reed Neil Olsen, and David M. Mitchell argue that mammals, birds, amphibians, insects, and even plants are affected by light pollution.[3]

The three Missouri State professors point to the disruption of migratory patterns of nocturnal birds and the disorientation of hatchling sea turtles that results in their demise. Additionally, they emphasize that human physiology is not immune to the problem of light pollution. They cite a 2001 study that refers to an increased risk of breast cancer in women with lower levels of melatonin production due to light pollution.[4] The problem is that light pollution keeps humans from falling into a deep sleep, resulting in less melatonin production.

State, National, Global Issue

The three Missouri State University professors cite studies that show that 66 percent of U.S. residents and 50 percent of the European population can no longer see the Milky Way at night. Also, about 40 percent of U.S. residents and almost 20 percent of the European Union population have lost the ability to view the night sky with eyes that can readily adapt to its darkness. Put simply, they cannot really experience nighttime.[5]

A global organization that is intent on reducing the luminous fog that increasingly envelopes populated areas of the Earth is known as the International Dark-Sky Association (IDA). Members of IDA explain that their nonprofit organization fights to preserve the night, with the benefits of protecting wildlife, cutting energy waste, and curbing light pollution. IDA's engineers and scientists provide home owners and business owners with advice on efficient and effective lighting.

Attorneys and public policy experts with the International Dark-Sky Association provide consultation on how to craft commonsense legislation to cut down on light pollution. To dramatize their cause, members of IDA have sponsored dark-sky evenings when lights are to be dimmed or extinguished. The organization claims about five thousand members in seventy countries around the globe.

Light Pollution Q & A

Robert Wagner of Kansas City answers a few questions about light pollution's effects. He was the International Dark-Sky Association (IDA) president in 2010. IDA works to protect and preserve the night sky.

Q. How many states or cities have enacted light pollution laws? What would be the most common rationale for such restrictions?

A. Several thousand cities now have light laws. One of the primary purposes of ordinances is to try to come up with a set of rules that everyone can live by—keeping one neighbor from intruding on another. Glare and lights shining into windows at night are seen as a major annoyance and most cities work hard to listen to people and to try to come up with some rules to limit such intrusion.

Q. What do we lose psychologically because of light pollution? What health issues might be attributed to it?

A. Psychologically—I think we are taking something precious from future generations. A night under an unspoiled firmament provides us with an opportunity for self-reflection and a deeper understanding of our place in the cosmos. Left in a man-made environment, we lose a bit of religion and a piece of our soul.

Q. Is it an exaggeration to say that insects, birds, and fish suffer from light pollution? Do we not have dominion over these creatures, and if they have to endure some urban light, so be it?

A. The research is fairly conclusive that animals, which evolved to natural nighttime illumination levels, are impacted by artificial lighting. How is our quality of life impacted by extinction and eradication of nighttime animals? Will we be better when there are no longer any moths to pollinate our crops at night? No bats to eat mosquitoes?

Q. "Sustainability" seems to be replacing "environmentalism" as the key word in learning how to live in sync with the planet. How does addressing light pollution contribute to sustainable living?

A. A natural nighttime environment is essential for our long-term coexistence with nature. Fixing light pollution allows us to improve both our quality of life and the ecosystem around us.

Notes

1. Logan, Lee, "Missouri Legislation Would Limit Light Pollution," *Columbia Missourian* (Feb. 2, 2009): 1-2, www.columbiamissourian.com/a/110571/missouri-legislation-would-limit-light-pollution.
2. Ibid.
3. Gallaway, Terrel, Reed N. Olsen, and David M. Mitchell, "The Economics of Global Light Pollution;" paper presented at Western Economic Association; Section II: Externalities and Light Pollution (August 2009).
4. Ibid.
5. Ibid., Section I: Introduction.

Additional Readings

International Dark-Sky Association Staff, *Fighting Light Pollution: Smart Lighting Solutions for Individuals and Communities* (Mechanicsburg, Penn.: Stackpole Books, 2012).
Mizon, Bob, *Light Pollution: Responses and Remedies* (Myrtle Beach, S.C.: Springer Press, 2001).
Rich, Catherine, and Travis Longcore, *Ecological Consequences of Artificial Night Lighting* (Washington, D.C.: Island Press, 2005).

DECIBEL POLLUTION
WHEN EARS DO NOT HEAR

Photo by
Courtney Martin

M issourians living in Kansas City have benefited from a wide-ranging noise control ordinance that covers everything from power drills, chain saws, sanders, lawn mowers, radios, televisions, drums, guitars, security alarms, and more. St. Louis also has a detailed noise control ordinance. However, beyond Kansas City and St. Louis, most suburban cities and rural towns in Missouri lack such citizen protections.

According to the Kansas City ordinance, "Citizens of the city have a right to and should be ensured an environment free from excessive sound that may jeopardize their health or welfare or safety or degrade the quality of life."[1] The Kansas City ordinance includes tables with specific decibel level limits. Noise or sound is calibrated in decibels (db) and generally follows a scale from the 30 db of a whisper to the very painful 120–140 db of a jackhammer or a rock concert.

A person's hearing can be damaged by lower levels of noise depending on the length of exposure. Eco-Healthy Child Care points out that vacuum cleaners and other household appliances operate at 60 to 80 db. Brief exposures to such levels may be safe, but over a prolonged period of time these levels can start to cause harm.[2]

Beyond Missouri's two urban centers, harmful effects of noise pollution have been recognized by the EPA and the World Health Organization (WHO). The U.S. Centers for Disease Control and Prevention (CDC) tags noise pollution as "an increasing public health problem" with adverse effects ranging from high blood pressure and severe headaches to hearing loss and mental health impacts.[3]

Disturbing the Commons

Noise Pollution Clearinghouse (NPC) and NoiseOff (Coalition Against Noise Pollution) are among a number of activist groups that have raised their voices, albeit at moderate decibel levels, to sensitize Americans to their natural auditory rights. NPC notes that the word *noise* derives from the Latin term "nausea," which means "seasickness."[4] NPC documents how ear passages full of noise from boom boxes, jackhammers, or jet skis can render a person dazed, dizzy, damaged—and nauseated.

NPC takes the view that the air surrounding us is part of the "commons" and belongs to no individual or business, but to all of us. We therefore have the right to demand limits to the audible litter others may try to dump on our common areas. "We have a right to raise awareness of noise pollution and help communities take back the commons from those acting like bullies," the NPC declares.[5]

NoiseOff offers moral support to all scientists, engineers, pundits, authors, and grassroots activists who refuse to turn a blind eye or a deaf ear to those violating the commons with excessive racket. For example, it lauds "PIPEDOWN Newsletter" for promoting the campaign for freedom from piped music. NoiseOff gives rave reviews to the book, *Why Noise Matters: A Worldwide Perspective on the Problems, Policies and Solutions*, which showcases legal policies and strategies that have worked to decrease noise pollution. It gives kudos to police chiefs who enforce noise codes by pulling over drivers who crank up the stereo while cruising America's streets.

Noise Free America

Noise Free America (NFA) insists that noise is intrusive and harmful and cites the words of former U.S. Surgeon General William H. Stewart, who stated: "Calling noise a nuisance is like calling smog an inconvenience. Noise must be considered a hazard to the health of people everywhere."[6]

Founded by a group of students at the University of California–Los Angeles in 2001, NFA issues the "Noisy Dozen" award, which has been bestowed on such cities as Washington, D.C., and Youngstown, Ohio.[7] Noise Free America has a number of engineers in its ranks who are happy to act as a sounding board for technical questions about noise. Indeed, one of them, Ruth Schiedermayer, has been enlisted for the question-and-answer exercise here.

Noise Pollution Q & A

Ruth Schiedermayer answers a few questions about noise pollution. She joined the Institute for Noise Control Engineering (INCE) as an associate member interested in community noise, industrial noise, and the perception and effects of noise. She is an automation engineer by profession.

Q. What is noise pollution? Why is noise not just a nuisance but an environmental issue?

A. Several researchers have studied the impact of anthropogenic noise in recent years. Marine noise including sonar, which has been on the rise, has been shown to affect whales and dolphins and other sea creatures. Studies have linked increased noise levels to higher hypertension levels in humans. Much of current research concerns transportation noise. I read a rather elegant study of sleep cycles versus noise levels in the *INCE Journal* a couple years back. The conclusion was that even though people appear to not notice noise, there is a measurable change in depth/quality of sleep based upon background noise.

Q. OSHA (Occupational Safety and Health Administration) determines noise safety standards by decibel (db) levels and duration of time a worker is exposed to noise. Is eight hours of 90 db level worse than four hours of 95 db level noise?

A. As I understand it, the answer is no as these are hearing conservation guidelines for determining exposure level and duration versus potential hearing loss damage. They are of equal concern. Job safety training now often incorporates not just on-the-job hearing protection, but recommendations by the safety trainers about protecting one's hearing off the job.

Q. Should devices such as lawn mowers, leaf blowers, and chain saws have required labeling that indicates health hazards from exposure to the noise that they make?

A. The Noise Pollution Clearinghouse in conjunction with Consumer Reports did a study on lawn mowers. They rated several models including gasoline powered, electric, and "reel" or push mowers by measuring the noise levels. The conclusion was that most commercially available lawn mowers should be used with hearing protection. The need to require labeling is an issue to be discussed. Something like the Energy Star program might make the best sense. I know from private conversations that simply providing labeling of expected noise emissions of products throughout their life cycle might encourage the consumer to select quieter products.

Notes

1. Kansas City, Missouri, Chapter 46, Noise Control Code, p. 1, www.nonoise.org/lawlib/cities/kansascity/index.htm.
2. Staff Report, "Noise Pollution" (Washington, D.C.: Eco-Healthy Child Care, 2010): 1-2.
3. Ibid.
4. Noise Pollution Clearinghouse Staff, "About Noise, Noise Pollution, and the Clearinghouse," 1. See: www.nonoise.org/aboutno.htm.
5. Ibid.
6. Noise Free America Staff, "How to Fight Noise: A Guide to Reducing Community Noise Pollution" (Albany, New York, 2010), 4.
7. Noise Free America, noisefree.org/askanexpert.php.

Additional Readings

Cherian, Saneesh, and Philip Johnson, *How Noise Can Kill You* (Braintree, Ma.: Philip Communications, 2013).

Inseth, Zachary, *Noise Pollution: Earth's Conditions* (North Mankato, Minn.: Child's World Publishers, 1998).

Singal, S. P., *Noise Pollution and Control* (New Delhi, India: Narosa Publishing House, 2000).

Section 6

SHOW-ME
SUSTAINABILITY

Photo by
Courtney Martin

> *"The concepts and insights of the ecologists are of great usefulness in our predicament. And we can hardly escape the need to speak of 'ecology' and 'ecosystems.' But the terms themselves are culturally sterile. They come from the juiceless, abstract intellectuality of the universities. . . . The real names of the environment are the names of the rivers and river valleys; creeks, ridges and mountains; towns and cities; lakes, woodlands, lanes, roads, creatures and people. "*
> —Wendell Berry
> "Conservation Is Good Work," 1992

L egendary conservationist Wendell Berry is absolutely correct when he insists that we should not get too caught up in abstractions and sterile terminology when talking about the need to save our lakes, our woodlands, our creatures. On the other hand, words like *ecology, environment,* and *sustainability* are critical to working out a strategy for making a state, a country, or a planet a better place to live. Unfortunately, some key vocabulary of environmental science and nature study has come under attack in recent years.

When lecturing in outstate Missouri, it is a wise and useful tack to refer to oneself as a conservationist rather than as an environmentalist. Politicians and pundits have turned the term *environmentalist* into a dirty word. Likewise, "climate change" has taken the place of "global warming" as a slightly less offensive descriptive for what ails the planet. Even the vanilla term *sustainability* is under attack these days as the subversive verbiage of a United Nations conspiracy to deprive Americans of liberty as well as every modern convenience.

My hunch is that "sustainability" is here to stay, despite the ad hominem attacks and the suspicions of conspiracy buffs. That is because so many young people have embraced sustainable living, whether it involves energy use, personal transportation, or backyard gardening and ecology. Their fervor for conserving energy and finding alternative energy sources affirms their very real commitment to sustainability. So does their enthusiasm for biking to work when feasible or, at least, pedaling for recreation on an expanding network of trails. So does their experimentation with raising chickens, or creating rain gardens on their property, or growing organics in their own backyard plots.

This final section is the most positive portion of the book, and perhaps that is because sustainability is simply the most individual and promising approach to environmentalism. Too often, environmentalists seem entirely focused on the business of muckraking, detailing outrages, and outing transgressors. That is a bad rap and not an entirely accurate portrayal. Nevertheless, advocates of sustainability do seem more inclined to put the emphasis on problem solving and personal responsibility. And part of their problem-solving mission is manifest in their enthusiasm for providing "green education" for future generations.

DIAPER PARTIES
WITH MRS.
SUSTAINABILITY

Photo by
Courtney Martin

M ound City happens to be just one of many monikers for St.
Louis, a city in a region once dotted by mounds built by Native Americans. Those earthen mounds may be gone, but
new ones consisting of tons of garbage now have sprouted
across the local landscape. On the other side of the state,
the Kansas City area also boasts some monumental landfills that tower over
field and stream.

Within the waste layers of these landfills: ton upon ton of dirty, disposable diapers. Statistics on dirty diapers are not for the faint of heart or the delicate of nose. In a home with a baby in disposables, up to 50 percent of the household waste comes from soiled diapers.[1] More than 90 percent of those single-use diapers end up in landfills.[2] Instructions on the packages of disposables advise that all fecal matter should be dumped into the toilet before depositing the diaper in the trash, but less than one-half of 1 percent of all waste from single-use diapers actually makes it into the sewer system.[3]

Had enough? Here are a few more stinking statistics: disposable diapers rank as the third-largest consumer item contributing to the nation's growing landfills.[4] Disposable diapers decompose according to their location within the mountains of rubbish, but it is a safe bet that total decomposition takes about 250 to 500 years. Diapers dumped in a landfill on the day you are reading this will still be around when your great-great-great-grandchildren have passed from this earth.

Party On—with Cloth Diapers

Alarm over diaper-laden landfills has spawned a new phenomenon known as Diaper Parties. Two mothers who have enlisted in the cause of recyclable, cloth diapers are Laura Hammond of Missouri and Megan Blind of Illinois. They are state and regional consultants for Diaper Parties, and their mission is to preach the benefits of cloth and to get other mothers to make the switch like they did.

At their Diaper Parties, much like other home-based business parties such as Pampered Chef events, the women showcase a variety of cloth diapers. The parties offer an opportunity for guests to learn the benefits of cloth diapering and to try the diapers out on dolls, which are more manageable than the real thing.

"For me, it is mostly about education and helping people find the right diaper for them," Hammond told Julia Gabbert, an environmental writer in St. Louis. "This is something you can do for your child and the environment. . . . If you had to pile up six thousand disposable diapers in your backyard—an average baby's use—it would be a mountain for each child," added Hammond of Columbia, Missouri. "There are millions of babies in the world. We are going to run out of room eventually."[5]

Megan Blind agreed with Hammond and stressed that cloth diapers are all about healthier babies, a cleaner environment, home economics, and sustainable living. Blind said she is convinced that new mothers can reduce their carbon footprint in a big way through the use of cloth diapers.

Reusables Versus Disposables

Cloth diapers have environmental impacts that are often overlooked in a comparison of reusables versus disposables, according to a study by Wanda Olson, Sherri Gahring, and Thomas Halbach of the University of Minnesota Extension Service. They point out that a load of home-laundered diapers uses up to fifty gallons of water. Also to be considered is the energy used to heat the water and the negative effects of bleach and detergent chemicals used in washing.[6]

Hammond and Blind are sticking with their Diaper Party story. To cut down on the energy used for laundry appliances, there is cold water and washing by hand, according to Blind. She also said she relies on a clothesline and the sun to dry her cloth diapers. Solar power is always a nice piece of sustainability.

Diaper Parties Q & A

Megan Blind is a state and regional consultant for Diaper Parties.

Q. Diapering choice is said to be the most important environmental decision that parents with young children can make. Do you agree? How did you decide on cloth?

A. I do agree it is an important parenting decision. Disposable diapers have known carcinogens in them, which can directly impact children and their health. I started using cloth not only for the health aspect of it, but for the money-saving aspect. The great thing is parents do not even need to cloth diaper (CD) full-time. One diaper a day makes a huge difference for your baby, your wallet, and the environment.

Q. What about the yuck factor? Is dealing with a loaded cloth diaper a turnoff for parents who know that they can discard disposables quickly and with less mess?

A. When a baby goes #2 in a diaper, it can easily be dumped into the toilet, sprayed in the toilet—with a special spray attachment that hooks onto the toilet water lines—and there are even flushable and biodegradable liners that you can place inside the diaper and toss when soiled before putting the diaper into the washing machine.

Q. How about costs? Any idea on what kind of savings add up when you switch to cloth?

A. A child will go through about six thousand diapers in their first two years of life. If a child needs sixty diapers a week at about $.25 a diaper, the total cost equals out to $1,600 for just the first two years of a child's life. Families can CD their baby for as little as $300 total! And that savings can be taken over to the next child since they can be reused!

Q. Are there any health benefits for babies whose parents diaper them in the latest cloth diaper apparel as opposed to disposables?

A. There is a chemical in disposable diapers called dioxin. It is a known carcinogen that is banned in most countries; however, it is not in the United States. Also, disposable diapers can cause diaper rash as they leave moisture against baby's skin. CDs actually pull the moisture away, leaving baby's bottom dry.

Q. How much mileage can you get out of a cloth diaper? How many times can it be used?

A. Cloth diapers can be used for multiple children if taken care of properly. Diapers today are made out of polyurethane laminate or PUL. PUL is a waterproof backing that comes in tons of colors and designs.

Notes

1. Link, Ann, "Disposable Nappies: A Case Study in Waste Prevention," *Women's Environmental Network* (April 2003).
2. Lehrburger, Carl, *Diapers in the Waste Stream: A Review of Waste Management and Public Policy Issues* (Sheffield, Mass: self-published, 1988): 1.
3. Ibid.
4. Link.
5. Gabbert, Julia, "Diaper Parties," *Environmental Journalism* (February 2012): 1-2.
6. Olson, Wanda, Sherri Gahring, and Thomas Halbach, *Waste Education Series: Diaper Choices* (Minnesota: Extension Services Publishing, 2012), 3.

Additional Readings

Dolan, Deirdre, and Alexandra Zissu, *The Complete Organic Pregnancy* (New York: William Morrow, 2006).

Greene, Alan, *Raising Baby Green: The Earth-Friendly Guide to Pregnancy, Childbirth, and Baby Care* (San Francisco: Jossey-Bass, 2007).

Hatch, Joy, and Rebecca Kelley, *The Economical Baby Guide: Down-to-Earth Ways for Parents to Save Money and the Planet* (Bel Air, Calif.: Stewart, Tabori & Chang, 2010).

PACIFIC RING'S
MR. SUSTAINABILITY

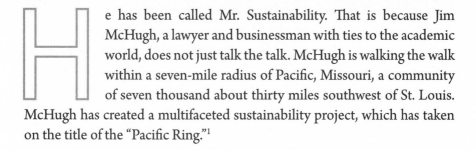

H e has been called Mr. Sustainability. That is because Jim McHugh, a lawyer and businessman with ties to the academic world, does not just talk the talk. McHugh is walking the walk within a seven-mile radius of Pacific, Missouri, a community of seven thousand about thirty miles southwest of St. Louis. McHugh has created a multifaceted sustainability project, which has taken on the title of the "Pacific Ring."[1]

As past president of the University of Missouri Board of Curators, a marketing executive with Hussmann Corp., an international business director for Pet, and a lawyer with Paule, Camazine & Blumenthal, McHugh had a Rolodex full of names of talented folks to help with his goal of implementing sustainability ideas. So what did his brain trust come up with? Here are just three of the ventures that they have started:

- *Beef Project*: This involves, in part, creating a grain feed business so that cattle do not have to be shipped to feedlots miles away from farms in the Pacific Ring. It also involves a system to process the cattle waste into natural gas to fuel the operation.

- *Coal Ash Project*: This involves finding a way to use all that coal ash from Ameren's Labadie electric plant for something more productive than a landfill. The idea is to combine it with silicon sand mined in Pacific to create a cement superior to the real thing.

- *Meramec River Project*: Part of the Pacific Ring is in a seemingly useless river floodplain. The idea here is to create an area for recreation, entertainment, and science study. This project is already under way with great help from many advocates for LaBarque Conservation Area destinations.[2]

Defining Sustainability

The term *sustainability* has become a buzzword, and it is sometimes difficult to arrive at a consensus on what it actually means. Generally, sustainability means management of the consumption of resources in a way that promotes healthy living, while at the same time ensuring that resources are not depleted and the environment is not degraded. Put simply: think responsible stewardship of the planet, which sustains us.

"Sustainable development is development that meets the needs of the present without compromising the ability of future generations to meet their own needs," according to the United Nations's Brundtland Commission in a 1987 report on the environment.[3] Since that report, a sustainability movement has gathered momentum, particularly among young people.

No one has captured the youthful enthusiasm for sustainability better than eco-author Lynne Cherry with her "Young Voices for the Planet" project. Her series of short films features young people using science and data to reduce the carbon footprint of their homes, schools, communities, and states. The films allow young voices to be heard on projects to reduce electricity consumption, to eliminate the use of plastics, to promote "green ambassadors," and more.[4]

Keep Sustainability Politically Neutral

The Pacific Ring's McHugh contends that the worst thing that could happen to sustainability is that it becomes politicized by the left or right wing in this country. He said sustainability should be a movement that promotes common-sense living and not a political agenda or a route to collecting votes in an election.

The most successful champions of sustainability, according to McHugh, will be those who can bring two disparate cultures together for the common good: academia and business. He said it is not always easy to get those who are in the "search for truth" and those who are in the "search for profit" to see eye to eye. However, a growing sustainability movement offers a nexus where the two cultures can meet.[5]

Pacific Ring Q & A

James L. McHugh is the creator of the sustainability project "Pacific Ring." He is a lawyer with Paule, Camazine & Blumenthal.

Q. **What is the Pacific Ring project, and what are some of the sustainable ideas that are being brought to reality? How can it be duplicated elsewhere?**

A. The Pacific Ring is a sustainable community project. We are defining sustainability through a proof of concept. The Pacific Ring is the area within seven miles of the City of Pacific. The first steps can be taken with any area, regardless of location. We accessed all the resources within this area, from population, businesses, natural resources, etc. We then tried to identify the absolute advantage and the comparative advantages within the area, using the results to select the projects guided by these advantages.

Q. **Sustainability is all the rage among many college kids these days. How does a fellow your age get on board the sustainability movement at this point in life?**

A. Our initial model (of sustainability) was illustrated by what we called a "sustainable triangle" with environmental policy on the bottom and moving up through air and water quality, and other variables like health care, education, etc., with the economy at the top. We ended up inverting this triangle and putting the economy at the bottom based on the belief that people will not seriously think a lot about environmental issues unless they have jobs and the basic necessities.

Q. **You have said that sustainability is, in part, about creating jobs that are not at the expense of the environment. Is that really possible when it comes to fracking for natural gas or developing oil shale deposits?**

A. Sustainability is good business, but this calls for an education process. If you want a perfect world with a natural environment not altered or affected by humans, you cannot tolerate our presence on this planet. Of course there may be some adverse effects from fracking, use of coal, oil and gas, but the use of these resources must be balanced against the benefits—namely a sustainable economy. Timing is the most important thing in balancing economic interests with the emergence of new technology, e.g., wind and solar.

Q. Missouri has a reputation for being a backwater when it comes to environmental sensitivity and promoting models of sustainability. Is this reputation deserved and, if so, can that situation be changed?

A. I am not sure that Missouri deserves this reputation. When we began suggesting sustainable practices to the small farms in the Pacific Ring, they were initially insulted, explaining that they have been engaged in these practices for many years. That is why the opportunities are so great, because I think many of us would be surprised how well the public is informed and knowledgeable about conservation and sustainable issues. They do not call it "sustainability" but "survivability."

Notes

1. Corrigan, Don, "Webster's Jim McHugh Heads Pacific Ring Project," *Webster-Kirkwood Times* (March 16, 2012): 1, 8.
2. Ibid., 8
3. United Nations General Assembly, "Report of the World Commission on Environment and Development: Our Common Future" (March 20, 1987).
4. Savedge, Jenn, "Young Voices on Climate Change," *Mother Nature Network* (January 26, 2011); See also: "Lynne Cherry," Contemporary Authors Online (October 11, 2006): 1-2.
5. Corrigan, 8.

Additional Readings

Braungart, Michael, and William McDonough, *Cradle to Cradle: Remaking the Way We Make Things* (New York: North Point Press, 2002).
Dresner, Simon, *The Principles of Sustainability* (New York: Routledge, 2008).
Edwards, Andres R., and David W. Orr, *The Sustainability Revolution: Portrait of a Paradigm Shift* (Vancouver, Canada: New Society Publishers, 2005).
Hawken, Paul, *The Ecology of Commerce Revised Edition: A Declaration of Sustainability* (New York: HarperCollins, 2010).

GREENING HOMES
SUFFICIENTLY
EFFICIENT

Photo by Diana Linsley

G reenhouses used to be glass-pane buildings with climate-controlled interiors that kept constant levels of humidity and temperature. These environments are perfect for raising tropical plants, finicky fruits and vegetables, or decorative flowers. Today, a "green house" might also be an energy-efficient home for humans with an environmental bent or just a yearning for cost savings.

Today's green houses can be built from scratch or they can be older structures retrofitted with new materials and appliances that make them "green." For example, skylights can be installed in interior rooms to reduce electricity use during the daytime. Solar panels on roofs can provide most of a home's electricity and end reliance on energy from fossil fuels. Old windows and doorframes can be replaced with new designs that leak far less air from home heating and cooling units.

So-called gray water systems can recycle water used in sinks and showers, redirecting it to quench thirsty gardens.[1] Outside the house, water management can be a key component for an eco-friendly dwelling. Impervious surfaces, such as driveways, can be minimized. Rain barrels can catch water running off roofs that would otherwise cause erosion and swell local streams and waterways.

Retrofitting Does Not Cost, It Pays

Jim and Judy Stroup of South St. Louis County retrofitted their home from top to bottom. They installed a geothermal heating and cooling system that uses an earth loop to supply air needs for every season. They use low-energy LEDs (light-emitting diodes) for their lighting requirements. They have updated attic insulation to replace the original material that had settled into a mush between the attic support beams.

The Stroups decided to have MicroGrid Energy, a Missouri-based solar company, install solar panels in 2012. The installation has dramatically reduced their electric bills and their excess capacity goes to the Ameren electric utility grid. Jim Stroup said he now spends more on beer and pistachios than he does on gas and electric.

The Stroups got more than a little help for their solar energy system's costs, including a 30 percent federal tax credit and a solar renewable energy credit from Ameren, as well as a rebate from the utility company. With all that help, the system will pay for itself with the reduced electric bills in about five-and-a-half years.[2]

Judy Stroup said that she and Jim talked to neighbors about the roof installation to make sure there were no concerns about "the look" of it:

"The solar panels are dark and just not that noticeable. What amazes me is that even when it is a cloudy day, some electricity is produced. We have a connection to our computer, so we can actually monitor what it is doing any time of day."[3]

Building New: Lean and Green

Missouri has not had the best track record nationally for building new green homes. However, St. Louis is on a rapid pace for improvement. For example, Habitat for Humanity in St. Louis now builds all of its homes to five-star energy standards, with donated materials and 75 percent volunteer labor.[4]

Another bright, energy-efficient spot: St. Louis now has the second-highest number of LEED (Leadership in Energy and Environmental Design) platinum homes, the highest standard for green building, according to Jean Ponzi of the St. Louis EarthWays Center.[5]

Green builder James Trout observes: "In construction, one of the stricter green standards is LEED. The Home Builders Association (HBA) came up with a more streamlined version called Green Building Standard that mimics LEED, but is considered more user-friendly and affordable. The future will be an affordable, verifiable marriage of the two. Branding aside, green typically means conscientious attention was paid to the efficiency and renewability.

"A house is a system, and the more holistically planned, the better for the occupant, the checkbook and the planet," contends Trout. "A companion issue is the perceived value: Am I building energy equity? Extending the life of my abode? Extending as well the life of my planet?"[6]

Building Green Q & A

James Trout created the Indoor Air Quality Policy for the Governors Council on Disability in Missouri and is a green designer/builder and consultant in St. Louis.

Q. It has been asserted that homes built green are not vulnerable to termites, carpenter ants, rot, dry rot, and mold. Since St. Louis is known for these sorts of home wreckers, is that not a bold claim to make?

A. Of course it is bold. It is also possible if executed properly. Two ways: use building materials that are more natural and sustainable, and handle moisture, fresh air, and gas-off differently. When you get the materials and moisture right, termites and mold will move on. Green to me includes a safer home.

Q. What are/is the most important among the elements that make a green home?

A. A house is a system, and the more holistically planned the better for the occupant, the checkbook, and the planet. The focus is on a few simple issues. First is recycling: if you restore a building versus building new, you are way ahead of the game. The second might be air quality: controlling the air changes per hour, moisture, and gas-off from the materials used. Systems: how much energy is consumed to produce a standard benefit (lighting, cooling, etc.).

Q. In terms of building or buying these kinds of homes, what help is available from federal programs such as Building America and Energy Star Homes or EEM, Energy Efficient Mortgage?

A. Places like DSIREusa.org or MyGreenToolkit.com can plug us into specials on credits and grants. Watch for one available to commercial buildings now, called PACE, [which] will grow to the residential market in a year or two. See MoPACE. wordpress.com for how this thing works—it is a game changer: Borrowing against your future property taxes for alternative energy improvements that will save you more than you spend.

Q. What are some examples of where people have gone wrong in trying to build green and energy efficient?

A. I once worked in a government LEED platinum building where workers were cooked by "daylight harvesting" and needed buses for the half-mile trek from the parking lot to the building every day so landscapes could drain rainwater without pipes. Sometimes, if only the green geek is given the keys to the planning room; then things can become obsessively one-sided.

Q. If you try to retrofit a home to be green and energy efficient, where do you start?

A. You start with a Building Performance Institute, Inc. (BPI) audit, which is cheap by most standards and readily available and absolutely necessary. It provides the exact identity of the culprits, goes beyond the usual suspects, and recommends improvements in order of return on investment. It pays for itself in about a month.

Notes

1. Farghalli, Nancy, "Recycling 'Gray Water' Cheaply, Safely," National Public Radio (June 8, 2009).
2. Corrigan, Don, "Living Green With Solar Energy," *Webster-Kirkwood Times* (Dec. 14, 2012): 16-17.
3. Ibid.
4. Schuessler, Todd, "St. Louis Green Status," *Environmental Reporting* (April 30, 2012): 1-3.
5. Ibid.
6. Trout, James, email interview with Don Corrigan, July 3, 2012; see also JamesTrout.com.

Additional Readings

Chiras, Daniel, *The Solar House: Passive Heating and Cooling* (White River, Vt.: Chelsea Green Publishing, 2002).

Johnston, David, and Scott Gibson, *Green from the Ground Up: Sustainable, Healthy, and Energy-Efficient Home Construction* (Newtown, Conn.: Taunton, 2008).

Stang, Alana and Christopher Hawthorne, *The Green House: New Directions in Sustainable Architecture* (Princeton, N.J.: Princeton Architectural Press, 2010).

ALTERNATIVE ENERGY
GAINING POWER?

Photo by Diana Linsley

S hortly after the turn of the century, environmentalists and sustainability advocates began to see some success in their efforts to promote a "clean, renewable energy future." More than twenty-five states passed legislation setting targets to reduce electricity produced by fossil fuels and to increase the portion generated by wind, solar, and geothermal sources.[1] However, legislators in Missouri balked at the idea of setting up renewable energy mandates.

Consequently, groups such as Renew Missouri, Missouri Votes Conservation, Sierra Club, and the Missouri Coalition for the Environment put together a campaign to get a renewable energy standard on the ballot for voters to approve. They formed Missourians for Cleaner Cheaper Energy (MCCE), which collected signatures on initiative petitions and succeeded in getting a proposal on the state ballot.

In November 2008, Missouri voters passed Proposition C with an astounding 66 percent of voters approving Renew Missouri standards. These standards passed by voters require the state's publicly held utilities to generate 15 percent of their electricity from renewables by 2022.[2] Voters may have favored renewables, but the proposal's language immediately ran into trouble with the courts, the legislature, and the Public Service Commission.

Renew Missouri supporters were alarmed and disappointed to see state lawmakers start taking apart Proposition C beginning with their 2009 session. Among the actions taken: allowing utilities to pay for outsourced electricity from renewable sources in other states and allowing century-old hydroelectric plants to count as renewable energy sources. Both of these moves violate the spirit and intent of Proposition C, passed by voters in 2008.

Wind and Solar: Renewable Future?

Advocates for renewable energy sources point to wind and solar power as the pathway to end Missouri's heavy reliance on coal for energy production. They argue that wind and solar provide much cleaner electricity and also give consumers a cheaper source for electricity. They also point to other states where the push for renewables has not been resisted, but successfully implemented. These states are on track to meet renewable mandates and thousands of jobs have resulted from the new energy sector.[3]

Wind and solar are not without their skeptics. Spencer Abraham, U.S. Energy Secretary under President George W. Bush, insists that it is a misnomer to call these "renewables" because energy cannot be recycled. He also contends that wind and sun are not inexhaustible, reliable sources, because wind does not always blow and the sun does not always shine. Abraham leans toward nuclear energy as a clean, reliable energy source in his book *Lights Out! Ten Myths About (and Real Solutions to) America's Energy Crisis*.[4] However, his study was published before the Fukushima nuclear power plant disaster in Japan in March 2011, an event that blunted support for nuclear power.

Wind turbines are not the clean dream first envisioned by environmentalists, according to Abraham, because he maintains that windmill farms are unsightly and must be expansive to be effective. Abraham also takes aim at solar energy. He argues that for this source to be viable, huge solar collectors would have to be located in the desert Southwest. These would have to be supplemented by electrical storage technology and a total rewiring of America's energy grid to transport the energy from remote areas to urban centers.[5]

Renewable Energy: Sparking the Economy?

Nationally, renewable energy advocates took heart in 2010 when U.S. Department of Energy Chief Steven Chu gave a big boost to the National Renewable Energy Laboratory (NREL). The agency and its scientists were moved into the most energy-efficient buildings in America in Washington, D.C., and Colorado with displays to show off the latest renewable technologies under development. As Alexis Madrigal observed in his book *Powering the Dream: The History and Promise of Green Technology*, renewables experts finally had "the institutional support long enjoyed by nuclear power and fossil fuels in America."[6]

Closer to home, the energy picture in Missouri was not so bright. Alternative energy advocates in the state continued to point to much larger wind and solar energy investments in other states. They also debated whether to push for another statewide vote for a ballot measure containing precise language that could not be altered or ignored by state legislators.[7]

Renewable Energy Issues Q & A

Henry Robertson is a member of the Great Rivers Environmental Law Center who works on issues related to the Missouri Public Service Commission.

Q. Renewable energy includes biomass, burning methane from landfills or waste, solar panels, wind turbines, hydroelectric, and more. What forms of renewable energy make the most sense for Missouri?

A. Solar, wind, perhaps micro-hydro. Burning trash, wood, and even landfill gas creates pollution just like burning fossil fuels; "woody biomass" cannot be used at any large scale because there is not enough feedstock without deforesting the area.

Q. What is the problem with continuing to rely on traditional fossil fuels for generating electricity? Coal? Oil? Natural gas?

A. All increase the greenhouse effect, which is on course for runaway climate change. All are polluting in ways that are not fully controlled by pollution reduction technologies. Finally, they are in finite supply; even if reserves seem large, we are reaching the point where recovery becomes increasingly uneconomical. Fossil fuels are no longer cheap.

Q. The governor's office announced an initiative in spring 2012 to manufacture a new generation of smaller, mobile nuclear power plants. Can nuclear be the way to the future? And why do environmentalists not classify it as renewable?

A. Nuclear is not renewable because it depends on finite supplies of uranium. No solution has been found to the problem of radioactive waste storage; it must be safely sequestered for hundreds of thousands of years. The capital costs of nuclear are extremely high; there is a long history of cost overruns and the industry has always been heavily subsidized. These costs mean nuclear would crowd out investment in safer alternatives.

Q. How can people deploy renewable energy generation at home on a small scale? Is this the "ultimate in sustainability?" Or should people do more modest things, such as energy efficiency efforts?

A. Efficiency should be the groundwork for home renewables. The system must be sized to meet the home's needs, and will be much cheaper if those needs are reduced. Rooftop solar is quite attractive right now, but the sun goes down at night, so home owners still needs to draw power from the grid unless they go to the expense and trouble of a backup battery system.

Notes

1. Farber, Dan, "Is Michigan's constitution the right place for energy policy?" *Midwest Energy News* (November 10, 2012); www.midwestenergynews.com/2012/10/19/.
2. Corrigan, Don, "Missouri Clean Air Initiative Calls for Renewable Energy," *South County Times* (October 10, 2008): 1.
3. Michigan Public Service Commission, "Renewables Less Expensive Than Coal, Spark Economy"; see full report: www.michigan.gov/mpsc.
4. Abraham, Spencer, *Lights Out! Ten Myths About (and Real Solutions to) America's Energy Crisis* (New York: St. Martin's Press, 2010), 130-151.
5. Ibid., 152-161.
6. Madrigal, Alexis, *Powering the Dream: The History and Promise of Green Technology* (Cambridge, Mass.: Da Capo Press, 2011), 103-116.
7. Renew Missouri, Past Featured Articles, www.renewmo.org/in-the-news.html.

Additional Readings

Freese, Barbara, *Coal: A Human History* (Cambridge, Mass.: Perseus Publishing, 2003).
Krupp, Fred, *The Sequel, The Race to Reinvent Energy and Stop Global Warming* (New York: W.W. Norton, 2008).
Scheer, Hermann, *The Solar Economy: Renewable Energy for a Sustainable Future* (London: Earthscan, 2007).
Sweet, William, *Kicking the Carbon Habit: Global Warming and the Case for Renewable and Nuclear Energy* (New York: Columbia University Press, 2006).

RAIN GARDENS AND RAIN BARRELS, OH MY!

When it rains in St. Louis and Kansas City—and all points in between—it often has a tendency to pour. On September 12, 1977, Kansas City was hit with seventeen inches of rain and the runoff transformed a little stream called Brush Creek into a raging torrent.[1] The famous Country Club Plaza went underwater and twenty-five people died. More than $100 million in damages resulted.[2]

After the catastrophe, Brush Creek was reconfigured along with massive infrastructure improvements. However, the need to enlist individual citizens in regional storm water management to control runoff still remained. In 2006, green groups, government entities, and the local media rolled out the "10,000 Rain Gardens Initiative." The idea was to encourage home owners to create rain gardens, not only to slow water runoff from properties, but also to improve the quality of water draining off the Kansas City landscape.

The "10,000 Rain Gardens Initiative" inspired other green approaches to dealing with storm water, including vegetation buffers to protect wetlands, tree planting, rain barrel installations, and green roofs. A charitable program called "Green Angels" allowed individuals, businesses, and groups to donate funds to construct rain gardens for schools, nonprofit organizations, and neighborhoods.[3]

Rain Gardens and Rain Barrels

For the uninitiated, a rain garden is a planted depression that can look very much like a sinkhole. After an intense storm, the depressed area can come to resemble a small pond. Its purpose is multifold: to reduce runoff, to dramatically lessen flash flooding, to cut down on erosion, and to stem the amount of pollution reaching nearby creeks and streams. Rain gardens do best when they are edged with bushes, ferns, and small trees, while their interior "bowls" are planted with native plants tolerant of local climate, soil, and water conditions.

Rain barrels hark back to the days of cisterns in arid parts of America, when there was no tapwater, and water storage was essential for drinking and bathing. Today's rain barrels have been embraced by environmentalists. A good collection system can hold hundreds of gallons of rain from roof surfaces and save it from rushing into creeks and streams. The water can be redistributed more slowly through a drip hose or used for gardening.

New designs in rain barrel technology allow the vessels to be easily fitted to downspouts from roof gutters and are equipped with valves that allow them to drain completely in between showers and storms. Rain barrels do require some basic maintenance. They should be checked periodically for removal of sediment and algae growth. Also, they should be properly sealed at the top to make sure they do not become breeding grounds for pests such as mosquitoes.

A Good First Step

"Rain barrels are a good first step for getting into rain management on the property of your home," said Karla Wilson, project manager for the Deer Creek Watershed Alliance in St. Louis County. "It is a nice home addition and also a great symbol that you are going green. Having rain barrels can get the neighborhood talking about what you are up to. It generates lots of interest in the whole idea of harvesting rainwater."[4]

The Deer Creek Watershed Alliance has joined with other agencies in the St. Louis area in a program very similar to Kansas City's "10,000 Rain Gardens Initiative." The alliance, along with the Missouri Department of Natural Resources, Missouri Botanical Garden, and other entities, started a RainScape Rebate program in 2013. The RainScape program offers financial incentives and proven expertise to anyone interested in rain gardens and rain barrels to rein in the destructive force of storm water runoff.[5]

Rain Gardens/Rain Barrels Q & A

Scott Woodbury is the curator for the Whitmire Wildflower Garden at Shaw Nature Reserve in Missouri.

Q. Can you make a rain garden without an earthmover and some heavy equipment?

A. A small rain garden can be built in a day with a few friends and a shovel.

Q. When and why did Shaw Nature Reserve build its first rain garden?

A. We built our first rain garden at Shaw Nature Reserve about 2005 as a demonstration garden for home owners. We want to encourage home owners to use native plants in their landscape and try to showcase every opportunity for that.

Q. How does a rain garden differ from a retention pond?

A. A retention pond's main purpose is to catch rainwater and settle out sediment load while the water slowly evaporates or is drained to the next storm water feature. Rain gardens are designed to catch rainwater and slowly absorb the water back into the soil.

Q. Native plants are recommended for rain gardens, so they are tolerant of local climate. So what kind of plants do you choose for a climate as variable as Missouri's?

A. Although rain gardens are not a naturally occurring land feature, small depressions that hold water for a few days or hours after a storm have been a part of the landscape and native plants have evolved to live in these periodically wet places. Plants that can be found naturally in wet prairie seeps, river bottom floodplains, forest ponds, and wetlands all make good rain garden plants.

Q. Switching to the topic of rain barrels—do you need them if you have a rain garden? Or does a rain barrel have a totally different purpose?

A. Rain barrels are useful for capturing some rainwater from a rooftop to store it for later use, usually watering the garden. Both rain barrels and rain gardens are a way to store rainwater before it leaves your property, but they do not need to be used together. Many home owners direct their original runoff to a rain barrel and then capture all overflow with a rain garden.

Q. Rainwater is not advised for human consumption from rain barrels, so how should this water be used?

A. Rainwater is not safe to drink. Many pollutants are cleaned out of the air by rainwater like acid rain. Collected rainwater is ideal for watering your garden. Your plants will enjoy being watered with natural rain without all the chemicals that are added to make our drinking water safe for human consumption.

Notes

1. Corrigan, Don, *Show-Me . . . Nature's Wrath* (St. Louis: Reedy Press, 2009), 104-105.
2. Ibid.
3. Liveable Communities, "Sharing Stormwater Management Responsibilities," 1-4; see www.werf. org/liveablecommunities/studies_kc_mo.htm.
4. Corrigan, Don, "Residents Tout Benefits of Rain Barrel Use," *Webster-Kirkwood Times* (Feb. 1, 2013): 10.
5. Ibid.

Additional Readings

Dunnett, Nigel, and Andy Clayden, *Rain Gardens: Sustainable Rainwater Management for the Garden and Designed Landscape* (Portland: Timber Press, 2007).

Kraus, Helen, and Anne Spafford, *Rain Gardening in the South: Ecologically Designed Gardens for Drought, Deluge & Everything in Between* (Hillsborough, N.C.: Eno Publishers, 2009).

Novotny, V., and H. Olem, *Water Quality: Prevention, Identification, and Management of Diffuse Pollution* (New York: Van Nostrand Reinhold, 1994).

CLUCKING
OVER BACKYARD
CHICKEN COOPS

Photo by Ursula Ruhl

C
ity councils, town aldermen, and village trustees are used to dealing with zoning issues, but what about regulations for backyard chickens? Municipal officials are now grappling with ordinances about keeping chickens in the neighborhood. These officials endure lots of clucking and a few ruffled feathers over the issue, but chickens are not going to go away. That is because more and more of their citizens are turning to raising chickens as a sustainable practice and an environmentally sound approach to homegrown food.

"This whole chicken thing is new to me," said Cathy Forand, chairman of the trustees for Grantwood Village, Missouri, in 2011. "I just did not know that people were wanting to keep chickens in their backyard to have fresh eggs every day. It came to our attention when a chicken coop arrived at one of our resident's houses in August, and it got a neighbor upset."[1]

Forand is among hundreds of officials in St. Louis County and the state of Missouri who have had to do their homework on raising chickens in urban areas. She said that after much study, a proposed ordinance was put on the village website at grantwoodvillage.info to calm residents' concerns that the barnyard was coming to their backyards. The proposed ordinance drew from other cities' guidelines in putting together regulations on hometown henhouses.[2]

St. Louis County has more than ninety municipalities, and they have a patchwork of regulations on chickens. Many of them contradict one another. For Grantwood Village, rules for not allowing chickens to run at large were drawn from nearby Kirkwood and Sunset Hills. Wording that forbids raising chickens for commercial use was taken from Ladue. Limits on the number of chickens on any one property were determined by looking at cities comparable to Grantwood Village. No matter the limits and restrictions, chickens are catching on.

Why Chickens Are Catching On

Chickens are catching on because of a growing sustainability movement in this country. Sustainability on the home front means managing the homestead to meet or sustain your own needs as much as possible. That can mean solar panels on the roof for power, rain barrels under the downspouts for watering the garden, organic vegetables in the garden for wholesome food, and a chicken coop in the backyard for fresh, rich, tasty eggs every morning.

Raising backyard chickens makes sense from an environmental standpoint because of the increasing concern over food safety posed by large agribusiness operations. Advocates for sustainable lifestyles insist that monster-size flocks in commercial poultry production pose unacceptable health risks. Confined and overcrowded conditions cause stress and weaken the birds' immune systems.

Let us not be polite about raising feathery fowl—a by-product of the backyard phenomenon is chicken shit. Composting is the most desirable way to use the manure, neutralize smells, and convert it into useful fertilizer. Care must be taken to keep the compost away from slopes, ditches, and streams.[3] However, the task of dealing with backyard chicken waste is nothing compared to what giant concentrated animal feeding operations (CAFOs) must manage.

Urban Chicken Mythmaking

Some nasty misconceptions have arisen in response to the rage for backyard chicken raising. Author Patricia Foreman has outlined major concerns that she addresses in her, "7 False Myths About Urban Chickens." She takes them on, one by one, and describes them as: disease, noise, waste odor, attraction of rodents, property value decline, appearance issues. As city chicks grow in popularity, she addresses a final concern: what will the neighbors think?[4]

Perhaps the most pressing issue involves the media attention to avian flu outbreaks since the turn of the century. Foreman quotes directly from the Centers for Disease Control website on this count: "There is no need to remove a (family) flock of chickens because of concerns regarding avian flu." Foreman echoes environmentalists when she states that the avian flu threat comes from the enormous flocks raised in overcrowded conditions where they are fed the cheapest food possible.[5]

Backyard Chickens Q & A

Bill Ruppert raises chickens. He also owns the St. Louis office of National Nursery Products (NNP), which is a horticultural sales, marketing, and consulting company.

Q. How is backyard chicken raising better for the environment than just letting Tyson Farms or another farm factory do the job for us?

A. Small-scale keeping of any farm animals reduces concentrated enormous volumes of animal waste and impacts to the landscape. While large production agriculture is essential for feeding the worldwide masses, multiple small-scale animal keeping can assist with reducing some need for the large-scale operations.

Q. Why are you so high on the taste of home-fresh, backyard chicken eggs? What accounts for the better taste?

A. Fresh eggs are higher in moisture content, contributing to a full-bodied egg yolk and albumen in both substance and taste.

Q. What kinds of things do you avoid ingesting when you eat backyard chicken eggs compared to the factory farm eggs? Are there antibiotics or other feed contaminants that you avoid?

A. Keeping of small chicken flocks reduces the chances for disease outbreak and spread, thus eliminating the need for medicated feeds. Our flock is strictly fed with grain-based feeds with nutritional supplements.

Q. How do you responsibly dispose of the chicken manure as part of the sustainability approach to raising backyard chickens?

A. Our chicken manure is composted among other organic materials (leaves, grass clippings, straw, wood shavings, general garden waste), ultimately providing a nutritious and soil-structure-enhancing supplement.

Q. How did your childhood visits to your aunt and uncle's chicken coops in Pinckneyville, Illinois, influence your interest in backyard chicken raising? Was their operation "sustainability-oriented?"

A. As a child visiting their coop and flock, I enjoyed the discovery of fresh eggs— learning where eggs actually come from!—and the entertainment value of watching the social interaction of the hens. My aunt and uncle were a product of the Great Depression of the 1930s who lived sustainably in their daily lives. They taught me the value of capturing rainwater from the roof of the house for use in the garden and washing your hair!

Notes

1. Corrigan, Don, "Municipalities Tackle Regulation of Hometown Hen Houses," *Webster-Kirkwood Times* (November 11, 2011): 12-13.
2. Ibid.
3. Willis, Kimberly, and Rob Ludlow, *Raising Chickens for Dummies* (New Jersey: Wiley Publishing, 2009), 136-138.
4. Foreman, Patricia, "7 False Myths About Chickens," McMurray Hatchery Blog (January 13, 2011): 1; See www.mcmurrayhatcheryblog.com.
5. Ibid., 1.

Additional Readings

Litt, Robert, and Hannah Litt, *A Chicken in Every Yard: The Urban Farm Store's Guide to Chicken Keeping* (Berkeley, Calif.: Ten Speed Press, 2011).
Nelson, Norman, *Chicken Raising and Caring: A Beginner's Guide to Raising Your Backyard Chickens* (Amazon Digital Services, 2013).
Willis, Kimberly, and Rob Ludlow, *Raising Chickens for Dummies* (New Jersey: Wiley Publishing, 2009).

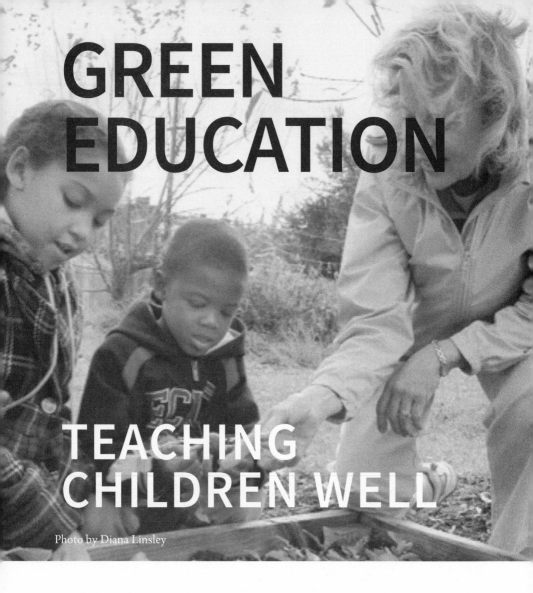

GREEN EDUCATION

TEACHING CHILDREN WELL

Photo by Diana Linsley

rosby, Stills, Nash & Young urged their baby boomer audience in 1970 to "teach their children well." Unfortunately, the flower-powered boomers, who enjoyed that song by Graham Nash, did not always do so well when they became parents. Too many of their children got their recreation at the shopping mall; got their "family time" at home in front of the wide-screen TV with their video games; and got most of their nourishment at fast food joints. What these kids did not get was fresh air.

This kind of unnatural lifestyle has a tendency to leave kids with barely passing physical health; below-par mental health; and sadly bereft of any vestige of imagination. Author Richard Louv describes this lamentable situation in his national best seller, *Last Child in the Woods: Saving Our Children from Nature-Deficit Disorder*. Louv attributes the sad condition of the young to what he describes as "nature-deficit disorder," a term which he has trademarked.[1] Louv argues that stress, passivity, depression, and obesity caused by nature-deficit disorder can best be addressed by simply getting kids into the woods—back to nature.

Of course, it is not really that simple. Kids these days need a little coaxing and some "green education" to appreciate what joys and benefits await them outside. Previous generations loved the outdoors and needed no persuading to dig in the dirt, climb a tree, build a treehouse, make a fort, or just go fishing. According to Louv, children now need some help to get "nature smart"[2] and to be reintroduced to the outdoors. He advocates eco-schools for the young and a new emphasis on ecological history and the resurrection of natural history at the higher education level.

Show-Me Nature Education Efforts

Missouri has no shortage of educators motivated to get kids into the woods for some outdoor learning. For example, the ShowMe Nature program in Columbia, Missouri, has sponsored numerous science safaris into natural habitats for grades K-12. The nature education program is a collaborative effort between the University of Missouri–Columbia and the Columbia public school system.

The Missouri Environmental Education Association (MEEA) sponsors programs across the state to get kids into the outdoors and to promote environmental literacy. MEEA has organized the Children in Nature Initiative that encourages rural, suburban, and urban school districts to all develop their own specific nature curriculum. MEEA has teamed up with the Missouri Bird Observatory, Gateway Children's High School Connection, and the Conservation Federation of Missouri to develop an environmentally literate citizenry.[3]

Schools in St. Louis are increasingly reaching out to nature. For example, Lindbergh High School has events with the Audubon Society and helps maintain a nature oasis called Claire Gempp Davidson Park. The College School in Webster Groves has acquired a twenty-eight-acre extended campus of woods, prairie, glade, meadow, bluffs, caves, and creeks in the LaBarque Creek area of Franklin County for the outdoor edification of College School students. Many schools have joined in green activities with the Green Center in University City, using its Kaufman Woods, Ozark Garden, and Roger Pryor Memorial Prairie Garden.

Kids and Families: Nature Activities

When an inventory is taken of all the schools, nature groups, and environmental organizations enlisted in the effort to counteract "nature-deficit disorder," it is apparent that a nature movement has formed. As Louv notes, it is a "movement fueled by this fundamental idea: the child in nature is an endangered species, and the health of children and the health of the Earth are inseparable."[4]

However, not all youthful nature activities should be part of an organized movement. Many nature activities should be do-it-yourself or family-based. Louv provides a useful list of ideas for exploration at the end of his book. They range from maintaining a birdbath to catching fireflies, as well as from building a snow cave in the winter, to cloud spotting in the spring, to hiking under a full moon in the summer. Talking up the nature movement is one thing, but it is also important to get out and do it.

Green Education Q & A

Jan Oberkramer is the executive director of the Green Center in University City where she coordinates and develops youth educational programming.

Q. Does nature education inevitably involve some lessons on sustainability issues and environmental responsibility?

A. In most cases. Hopefully, even the very young leave our programs with some sense of empathy and respect for plants and animals. We strive to engage children in the outdoors, develop a sense of connectedness, which leads to understanding and respect. I believe that most children who have multiple positive experiences in nature develop a natural stewardship.

Q. How would you describe some of the techniques used in nature education at the Green Center such as geocaching and letterboxing?

A. We try to find a balance between structured and unstructured programming and the use of technology. Letterboxing and geocaching speak to children's love for hunting treasure and also provide the opportunity for exploration. We have been using digital cameras in our "Connecting with Nature" program and the children love finding their own subjects to photograph and we find that they often "forget" their fear of nature in their excitement to capture a great photo op.

Q. How does nature education enhance sensory skills, such as sight, sound, taste, touch, and smell?

A. The natural world is experienced through the senses. It is inherently programmed into us to explore nature using our senses. Those who explore outdoors with me are usually subjected to quite a bit of tasting and I've noticed that younger children are most often the ones who reach out and touch the different textures of plants.

Q. What do we stand to lose if new generations continue to suffer "nature-deficit disorder" and a lack of appreciation for nature and the outdoors?

A. The most obvious loss would be to the natural world; our parks, wild areas, green spaces. It is nearly impossible for someone who has never or rarely interacted with nature to really understand or value the protection or stewardship of these areas.

Notes

1. Louv, Richard, "About Richard Louv," richardlouv.com/about/.
2. Louv, Richard, *Last Child Left in the Woods: Saving Our Children from Nature-Deficit Disorder* (Chapel Hill, N.C.: Workman Publishing, 2005), 203-204.
3. Missouri Children in Nature, "Why Should Missouri Children Get Outside?" childreninnature. mo.gov/about/.
4. Louv, *Last Child Left in the Woods*, 36, 371-387.

Additional Readings

Louv, Richard, *The Nature Principle: Human Restoration and the End of Nature-Deficit Disorder* (Chapel Hill, N.C.: Workman Publishing, 2011).
Orr, David W., *Ecological Literacy: Educating Our Children for a Sustainable World* (San Francisco: Sierra Club Books, 2005).
Selhub, Eva M., and Alan C. Logan, *Your Brain on Nature: The Science of Nature's Influence on Your Health, Happiness and Vitality* (New York: Wiley Press, 2012).

GREEN BURIAL
SUSTAINABILITY
AT TRAIL'S END

Photo by Courtney Martin

M ost committed environmentalists are too worried about planetary degradation—in the here and now—to care about what happens in their own futures. Most sustainability advocates also seem to be fixated on the viability of the here and now, rather than feeling concern for their own bodies at the end of life. There is a growing awareness, however, that a life dedicated to green ways should be celebrated and marked by sustainability efforts all the way to trail's end—thus, the rise of green burials.

Long before there was a green burial movement author Jessica Mitford took on the waste, decadence, and toxicity of the American way of death. As her many fans are fond of declaring, Mitford left no headstone unturned when she undertook her exploration of the business, sociology, and psychology of the funeral industry.[1] Mitford wrote *The American Way of Death* in 1963. Mitford went on to update her original work with *The American Way of Death Revisited*, which she completed just weeks before her own death in 1996. Her revised book appeared in bookstores in 1998.

Much of Mitford's work is focused on the consumer aspect of the process of disposing of the dead. She uncovers endless mendacity when it comes to the high prices of mortuary services, deluxe coffins, ubiquitous flowers, and vaulted grave sites. Her exposure of some of the monopoly practices in putting together end-of-life experiences actually inspired several legislative remedies in Congress.

Mitford was ahead of her time in the 1960s when she questioned the wisdom of embalming and dressing up corpses in costly, open caskets. After all, does the late, great Uncle Harry really need to be outfitted in his favorite suit and put on a padded casket mattress to rest his forever sedentary bones? Will the dearly departed Aunt Delilah feel disrespected if she is not dispatched in the Cadillac of crypts or planted in a square cemetery garden plot?

Sustainable Closure: Going Out Green

Most of us have a pretty good idea of what burial via the funeral industry is all about, but what is a green burial? According to the Reverend Charles Morris, an advisory board member of the Green Burial Council, green burials dispense with vaults, traditional embalming fluid, and heavy metal caskets.[2] In a June 2012 article in *National Catholic Reporter*, Reverend Morris explained that green burial caskets are of simple construction and built with sustainable materials such as bamboo or pine.[3] Because there is no vault, particularly with "shroud burials," there is the possibility of two bodies finding rest in one grave.

From an environmental standpoint, green burials release negligible greenhouse gases and the nutrients in bodies are recycled back to earth. Toxic chemicals are usually found in embalming fluids, including the known carcinogen formaldehyde. Steel caskets are often treated with finishes that are carcinogenic as well. Such toxics are avoided and there is less of an ecological footprint when going green versus the customary funeral industry burial.[4]

Monetary and Spiritual Benefits

At the end of the first decade of the twenty-first century, traditional funerals cost about $6,560, according to the National Funeral Directors Association.[5] A green burial costing half that amount caught America's attention with the 2008 economic downturn.

Reverend Morris argues that the American approach to bereavement began with the Civil War. Deceased Union soldiers' bodies were embalmed after battles for their return by train to families.[6] The origin of metal caskets can be traced to the one used to transport Abraham Lincoln's body across the country after his assassination. Caskets, vaults, and embalming are foreign practices in most of the world. Reverend Morris contends that the American way of death lacks an essential spirituality that can be recaptured with green burials where we can give ourselves back completely to God's earth. Reverend Morris notes: "Green burials, from my experience, are witness to the reality that we, indeed, are part of the creation and not apart from it."[7]

Green Burials Q & A

Joe Sehee is the founder of the Green Burial Council as well as an award-winning journalist and former Jesuit lay minister.

Q. How did you "think out" the concept of "green burials" and "sustainability at the end of life" from a philosophical standpoint?

A. I was involved with an early green burial project where things fell apart and it became pretty apparent to me that someone had to set forth verifiable standards if the concept was going to further legitimate environmental aims like protecting worker health, conserving natural resources, reducing carbon emissions, and preserving/restoring habitat.

Q. Jessica Mitford wrote a critique of the American way of death in her book by the same name. Where do you and Mitford find common ground when it comes to the commercialism and cost of traditional funerals and burials?

A. I really detest the commercialization of death care and the sales model that has been propped up, just like Mitford did. I think more people would embrace green burials if they knew they were dealing with professionals who had the psycho-socio and spiritual training to assist them in honoring the dead, healing the living, and inviting in the divine.

Q. Can you have a hybrid of traditional funeral and sustainable burial? Or are there certain criteria that really have to be met to make for a sustainable end of life?

A. We are dealing with enormously sensitive subject matter to begin with that is often complicated further by our religious beliefs and/or financial circumstances. What we (the Green Burial Council) have tried to do is to define the various environmental benefits of a green burial practice/product/facility so that consumers can make informed choices aligned with their core values.

Q. Have you presided over a funeral and burial using the "sustainability at the end of life" approach?

A. I have presided over a couple of funerals and one in particular really stands out for me. A three-year-old girl was killed by her mother in a botched attempted suicide/homicide that also caused brain damage to her older brother. The girl's father did not want a religious service. His parents, however, were first-generation Irish Catholics who very much were leaning on their god to get through this awful time. I was careful about not directly evoking god, but instead meditated on the concept of a fractal (a mystical pattern for life) inspired by a book I had read by a progressive Irish Catholic theologian/priest.

Q. Would funeral homes object to what you do with "green burials?" Or are they on board and willing to cooperate in the "sustainability at the end of life" approach?

A. Many funeral homes are still threatened by this idea like they are still threatened by cremation. We have been trying to find those folks in the field who are willing to do things differently and embrace a new ethic for a new era.

Notes

1. Mitford, Jessica, *The American Way of Death* (New York: Fawcett, 1983), 146-185.
2. Morris, Charles, "Green Burials Offer Ecological, Ancient Way to Say Goodbye to Loved Ones," *National Catholic Reporter* (June 21, 2012): 1-2.
3. Ibid.
4. Spitznagel, Eric, "The Greening of Death," *Businessweek* (November 3, 2011); www.business-week.com/magazine/the-greening-of-death-11032011.html.
5. Morris, 2.
6. Ibid.
7. Ibid.

Additional Readings

Leming, Michael R., and George E. Dickinson, *Understanding Dying, Death, and Bereavement* (Belmont, Calif.: Wadsworth Publishing, 2010).

Mitford, Jessica, *The American Way of Death Revisited* (New York: Vintage, 2000).

Roach, Mary, *Stiff: The Curious Lives of Human Cadavers* (New York: W. W. Norton & Company, 2004).

Schechter, Harold, *The Whole Death Catalog: A Lively Guide to the Bitter End* (New York: Ballantine Books, 2009).

Appendix: Useful Environmental Resources

The following listings are for environmental/conservation/nature groups and organizations that provide useful information for research purposes, op-ed commentaries, and letters to the editor in defense of our natural heritage. Many of these organizations were helpful with research material and advice for this book.

— Local Resources For Environmental Information —

ENVIRONMENT MISSOURI
www.environmentmissouri.org

FRIENDS OF OZARK RIVERWAYS
www.friendsofozarkriverways.org

FOREST PARK FOREVER
www.forestparkforever.org

GREAT RIVERS
ENVIRONMENTAL LAW CENTER
www.greatriverslaw.org

MARK TWAIN FOREST
WATCHERS
www.teaming.com/coalition-
organization/mark-twain-forest-
watchers

MISSOURI COALITION FOR THE
ENVIRONMENT
www.moenviron.org

MISSOURI ENVIRONMENTAL
EDUCATION ASSOCIATION
www.meea.org

MISSOURI PARK AND
RECREATION ASSOCIATION
www.mopark.org

MISSOURI PUBLIC INTEREST
RESEARCH GROUP
www.mopirg.org

NATURE CONSERVANCY OF
ST. LOUIS
www.nature.org

NORTH AMERICAN BUTTERFLY
ASSOCIATION OF ST. LOUIS
www.nabastl.org

RIVER DES PERES WATERSHED
COALITION
www.riverdesperes.org

ST. LOUIS AUDUBON SOCIETY
www.stlouisaudubon.org

ST. LOUIS GREEN
www.stlouisgreen.com

ST. LOUIS OPEN SPACE COUNCIL
www.openspacestl.org

ST. LOUIS SIERRA CLUB
ico.sierraclub.org/stlouis/getinvolved.
shtml

TRAILNET
www.trailnet.org

WEBSTER GROVES NATURE
STUDY SOCIETY
www.wgnss.org

— National Resources For Environmental Information —

AMERICAN LUNG ASSOCIATION
www.lung.org

AMERICAN RIVERS: RIVERS
CONNECT US
www.americanrivers.org

EARTH DAY NETWORK
www.earthday.org

ENVIRONMENTAL DEFENSE
FUND
www.edf.org

EVANGELICAL ENVIRONMENT
NETWORK
www.creationcare.org

GREEN PEACE
www.greenpeace.org

INTERNATIONAL DARK SKY
ASSOCIATION
www.darksky.org

IZAAK WALTON LEAGUE
www.iwla.org

NATURAL RESOURCES DEFENSE
COUNCIL
www.nrdc.org

NOISE FREE AMERICA
www.noisefree.org

NORBECK SOCIETY: DEEP
ECOLOGY
www.norbecksociety.com

RIVERKEEPERS
ENVIRONMENTAL PROTECTION
FOR WATERWAYS
www.riverkeepers.org

SIERRA CLUB
www.sierraclub.org

SOCIETY OF ENVIRONMENTAL
JOURNALISTS
www.sej.org

SUSTAINABLE
COMMUNICATIONS ONLINE
www.sustainable.org

TRUST FOR PUBLIC LAND
www.tpl.org

UNION OF CONCERNED
SCIENTISTS
www.ucsusa.org

WILDERNESS SOCIETY
www.wilderness.org

WORLD WILDLIFE FEDERATION
www.wwf.org